"Sheri's book articulates how God posi
in cities for his work. He planted Bı
help meet refugees' daily needs and perfect their walk in Christ.
Bridge of Hope's bibles enlightened our understanding of God's love
for his creation. Sheri always prayed for families, including myself,
which made me realize that Sheri cared for our walk in Christ
besides material. In 2012 after becoming a citizen, I wanted to visit
my country Uganda, but I did not have a warm jacket to endure the
long, stretched nights of flying. I contacted Sheri about needing a
jacket on my journey to Uganda. In just a few days, Sheri brought
me a beautiful, heavy, thick coat with an inner pocket to hide my
passport. This jacket was the best piece of clothing I have ever owned,
and today, it's the same jacket that I use when traveling between
states here in the USA.

I recommend ALL to read her book titled *Relentless Pursuit; God's
Gentle Guidance Amidst the Storm.* This book will bless you with an
immense knowledge of how God uses us and provides avenues to
sustain the needs of those that come to our shores."

—Womaniala Gerald
Community Leader, Licensed Driving school Instructor

"Sheri Briggs' story is a powerful testimony of God's intimate,
loving pursuit and the undeniable demonstration of his redemption.
Relentless Pursuit is personal, compelling and will both encourage and
challenge you. It will break your heart, give you hope and compel you
to respond to God's Relentless Pursuit!"

—Gina Stockton
Stockton Ministries
GinaStockton.com
The Sacred Space Podcast

"Sheri Briggs is one of my heroes! Her life is a testimony of God's redemptive power. I am so grateful that Sheri has written her story in this new captivating book because it is certain to release a gift of faith. As I read, I found myself thanking Jesus again for the very personal way he touches and shepherds his children. I am sure that this book will launch many on their own risk taking journey with God!"

—Robert Herber
Pastor, All Peoples Church San Diego
Leader, All Peoples Global

"In Sheri Briggs new book *Relentless Pursuit, God's Gentle Guidance Amidst the Storm*, you will find discovery and triumph from the incredible stories she shares. I know Sheri as "Mama Sheri" the founder of the Bridge of Hope SD, a ministry that strengthens families, by feeding and sheltering the poor and the destitute. She is full of love and compassion, and by reading this book you will find out what led to this life of her poured out service. Your view of the Father Heart of God will be forever changed by reading these pages."

—Bob Hasson Author *Shortcuts*,
Co-author *Wired to Hear* and *Business of Honor*,
CEO HPCI, Consultant.

"When you visit the Bridge of Hope, you are immediately welcomed into a dynamic, vibrant and eclectic community that loves and serves together. You might even say, you feel adopted into the new diverse family composed of immigrants from Uganda, Myanmar, Somalia, Syria and beyond, as well as many sojourners from San Diego seeking a true home. Sheri Briggs' gracious spirit born out of struggle and redemption is at the center of this exciting ministry. Her story, as recounted in these few pages, reveals how God uses small acts of faithfulness to reconcile and redeem creation, inviting us to be a part of the family of God."

—**Rev. Kevin Modesto**, Ph.D., MSW, MATS
Professor of Sociology and Social Work
Point Loma Nazarene University

"'Mama Sheri' first met me in the middle of my broken heart after losing our stillborn son, Nathaniel. She came with arms of compassionate love, sitting with me in my profound grief, unafraid of my questions or needs. As you read her compelling story and her tangible encounters with the person Jesus, you will receive this same invitation into wholeness. She demonstrates that there is no trauma, emotional, spiritual, or physical, that is beyond the reach of God's love. Her raw and vulnerable story, 'I wanted to hide in Him, like I always had, but I felt betrayed by Him. . . .' makes room for you to be seen and heard precisely where you're at. What areas of your life are the Father waiting to restore and redeem into something remarkable that is beyond your ability to imagine? This incredible read will invite you into the relentless pursuit that He has for your heart and your life. What if there is something waiting just for you that you were made to discover?"

—**Lauren Hasson**
Founder and Director of Lifestreams Ministries

"I recommend this book not only because it is an exciting and wild spiritual journey but also because the author practices what she preaches. You will be inspired, but also transformed by the work of the Holy Spirit through the life and ministry of Sheri Briggs."

—Kendall Laughlin, Jr
Pastor, Coach, and Author of *The Identity Journey*

"This book is a delight. Sheri Briggs has a compelling story and she tells it well. Sheri takes us on an adventure as she overcomes adversity and becomes better because of it. Vulnerable, powerful, each chapter convinces us God is there, personally engaged with us at all times, through both highs and lows. Reading this book will allow you to see the hand of God on her life – and yours – if you are looking."

—David I. Levy MD,
author of *Gray Matter: a neurosurgeon discovers the power of prayer . . . one patient at a time.*

RELENTLESS

God's Gentle Guidance Amidst the Storm

PURSUIT

SHERI ADAMS-BRIGGS

LUCIDBOOKS

Relentless Pursuit
God's Gentle Guidance Amidst the Storm

Copyright © 2022 by Sheri Adams-Briggs

Published by Lucid Books in Houston, TX
www.LucidBooks.com

eISBN: 978-1-63296-564-6
ISBN: 978-1-63296-563-9

This book is dedicated to my family.

To my faithful husband Brewster.

To my beautiful daughters, Emily and Lily.
May you know and live in the height and depth of God's love for you always.

To my beloved Nathan. I loved being your mama.
Thank you for being my son. I miss you every day.

I love you all with every fiber of my being.

Table of Contents

Foreword

Relentless Pursuit: God's Gentle Guidance Amidst the Storm is a life-enhancing gift to the world. Of all the life stories I have heard, none have impacted me more than Sheri's. Perhaps that is because her story came alive for me by experiencing the changed lives at the Bridge of Hope distribution center that she founded in San Diego, California. I witnessed people without clothes and food line up to receive abundant supplies, as Sheri and her volunteers gleefully and prayerfully ministered to both their physical and spiritual needs. I witnessed persecuted refugees from wartorn nations receive furniture, housing, tutoring, and Christian ministry.

It dawned on me that Sheri's struggles during her life had formed the pathway to her purpose in helping others. She writes about her own challenges in getting her personal needs met as a child who was raised in a cult, as a young mother in need of support, and how Jesus' example shows us how a person's physical needs must be met to create an opportunity for addressing their spiritual need for a loving God.

Not only is Sheri's story incredibly intriguing, but it is also compelling because of the depth of its meaning for each person who is privileged to know it. Reading this book will not only entertain you, but it will also cause you to reach into places few have traveled. I feel that there will be an impartation of Christ's grace to anyone who reads this book, and a motivation to fulfill the purpose to which God has called you.

My wife and I have come to know Sheri as a dear friend, and we have come to know Sheri's family as treasured friends as well. As an author of a book about Heaven, which was birthed from my own experience in Heaven after dying, I have come to know Sheri's story from a unique perspective. After her son Nathan journeyed to Heaven with Jesus forever, I remember trying to speak a word of encouragement to Sheri and her husband Brew. "He's so full of joy today in Heaven," I said. I can just imagine how trite those words must have sounded to a parent freshly in the throes of mourning. But then I heard Sheri speak at her son's memorial service, and she spoke with a depth of soul that could only have come from someone who knew the depth of God's love in broken places. When Sheri speaks to how God guides us through the storms of life, she speaks genuinely, experientially, and from a place of triumph.

Indeed, "the Lord is close to the brokenhearted" as the psalmist wrote in Psalm 34:18. God is very close to Sheri, and Sheri brings that closeness to her storytelling just as she does for the thousands who have been saved through her ministry; now, Sheri brings that closeness to the readers of Relentless Pursuit. She also brings an understanding of what it means to be raised in a place of spiritualism devoid of relationship and what a true relationship with people and with God should be for each of us. I love that Sheri writes from a depth of soul that can only be born through a life rich in rocky experiences and true discoveries. When you read this book, you will gain a greater depth of understanding along the journey of Sheri's incredible life. You may cry, you may laugh, you should be inspired, but you will most certainly be uplifted.

This book portrays an exceptional life with exceptional characters and situations that one might find in a great novel, but this is a true account. I love how Sheri tells her story with color and vibrancy and a rawness that draws the reader into a vicarious understanding of Sheri's profound life through the lenses of its humble author.

Relentless Pursuit lives up to its title and its author's amazing life. I also like the subtitle, God's Gentle Guidance Amidst the Storm, because it aligns with my experience in Heaven in meeting Jesus. During the storms of life, God guides us gently even when we miss His promptings. Sheri's telling of her story took courage, a strength steeled through trials, and a resolution evidenced by Sheri's profound ministry which supports countless families in crisis.

Enjoy this life-changing book because it was inspired through tears, laughter, and love. Relentless Pursuit finishes with Sheri's reward for her pursuit of God. Thank you, Sheri, for writing this love letter to God and to everyone who reads it.

Randy Kay

Founder, Randy Kay Ministries

Best Selling Author, *Revelations from Heaven and Dying to Meet Jesus*

Introduction

I had a conversation with a great writer and friend.

He asked, "Who are you writing this story to?

I am writing first to myself. I need to always remember what the Lord has done for me. It's a love story, and I need to hear it over and over again.

"He brought me [up] out of the pit of destruction, out of the miry clay, and He set my feet upon a rock, making my footsteps firm." Psalm 40:2. This truly is what has happened!

I share the story from the beginning, my childhood and early years, to show God's incredible love that brought me out of generational madness. He is the ultimate Father, and His love is bigger and stronger than anything we may face on this earth. He truly is the lover of our souls and stops at nothing to find us, heal us, and give us a future and hope.

"I am convinced nothing can separate us from the love of God; neither death nor life, nor angels, nor principalities, nor things present, nor things to come, nor powers, nor height, nor depth, nor any other created thing, will be able to separate us from His love." Romans 8:38-39

Early in my walk with the Lord, I felt led to study the Hebrew names of God. These names reveal who God is: His character, nature, and attributes. At the beginning of each chapter, I have highlighted two Hebrew names to show how God revealed Himself to me in that part of my story. His name frames each chapter, showing His overreaching sovereignty and love which overshadowed all that was happening in the natural.

"Some trust in chariots and some in horses, but we trust in the name of the Lord our God." Psalm 20:7

Because of who God is and my spiritual adoption, I am free from bondage. I have a beautiful family and a loving community of people around me. It is only because of Him that I could see through childhood deception and lies and heal from the effects of evil and sin. He is wisdom, and He has saved me and girded me with His strength. He has provided when there was no way. He has blessed me and exchanged beauty for ashes. He has walked with me in the valley of death and been the lifter of my head. He has never left me or forsaken me.

He is no respecter of persons the Bible says. This is who He is for all of us!

All of His goodness is what His name declares He is.

Another reason I wrote this book is for anyone who has a dream, a vision, or a calling.

Maybe you feel disqualified, unequipped, or you fear what others may think of your dreams or ideas, so you aren't taking action towards fulfilling your dreams. Maybe it feels like your dream is too big, far off in the future somewhere, or in the realm of impossibility. Maybe it seems unattainable because you don't know how you could fund it or imagine how it could possibly be done. All God dreams are God-sized and are not meant for you to make happen in your own strength or by your own means. This story is about faith, saying yes to Him and who His Word declares He is and stepping into where He leads you.

I hope and pray this book encourages you and fills your heart with courage to say yes to Him and the incredible journey He has planned for you!

Chapter 1
Crazytown

Yahweh, I AM

"And God said to Moses, 'I AM WHO I AM', and He said, 'This you shall say to the sons of Israel, "I AM has sent me to you"'
—Exodus 3:14 (NASB)

"Thine eyes have seen my unformed substance; And in Thy book they were all written, The days that were ordained for me, When as yet there was not one of them."
—Psalm 139:16

Yahweh Sali, My Rock/Hiding Place

The LORD is my rock, my fortress and my deliverer; my God is my rock, in whom I take refuge, my shield and the horn of my salvation, my stronghold.
—Psalm 18:2

"Sheri! Sheri! Wake up!"

"We've got to go! Hurry!"

"Get your shoes on! You don't have time to change . . . Just put a jacket over your pajamas."

Lying in my bed, I reached over to pull back the curtains, revealing the quiet of the night sky. *It couldn't possibly be time to get up for school already.*

"Quickly! We have to go. Now!"

Now, I was awake enough to have that familiar feeling–like someone had just sucker punched me in the gut, leaving me both frozen and nauseous. With my hair still in tangles and eyes half open, Mom rushed my brother Jimmy and me out of our rooms, down the stairs, and into the car.

It was 3 AM.

The seat felt like ice under my thin pajamas. Frantically, Mom drove us to her friend's house, dropped us off, and rushed off like a bat out of hell.

The explanation was all too familiar. Dad had gotten a flat tire on the freeway, and he needed Mom's help.

The truth was that Dad was driving drunk and had gotten picked up by the police. Mom was going to bail him out of jail, again. Feeling horribly awkward, my brother and I sat with forced smiles in the nice lady's living room, pretending this was all normal as we waited for Mom to return. The friend who agreed to take us in tried her best to make us feel comfortable by offering us a snack, but I felt too sick to eat. TV wasn't a good distraction either; it was too early to watch cartoons. It was awkward for everyone. We were supposed to be in bed, fast asleep.

Of course, Mom's friend knew what had happened. She acted strangely like she felt sorry for us.

Exhausted and unable to go back to sleep, my brother and I would miss school the next day.

This scene repeated itself over and over throughout my early childhood until my brother turned 16 and got his driver's license. That's when it was his turn to go alone and get Dad out of jail.

My parents were in crisis long before I came along and continued to be throughout my entire childhood. They met in college, both gifted musicians who were in the same music program at Pepperdine University. After they married, my mother taught kindergarten and my father became a middle school teacher, teaching music classes in Los Angeles.

While my mother was pregnant with my older brother, my father was convicted of a crime. I don't know many details, except for the creepy story Mom told me when I was in junior high school. To this day, I'm not sure what prompted her to tell me, but apparently, Dad was caught making obscene phone calls to women from random phone booths. At the time, I didn't know what an obscene phone call was. I remember wondering, *Is that like a prank call?* To this day, I'm thankful that I don't know the details of what he said. What I do know is that he had been making these calls for quite some time, and the detective on the case told my mom that in all his years in law enforcement, he had never heard such filth coming out of someone's mouth. He advised her to never listen to the tape recordings of my father. Criminal charges were filed against him, and he was banned from teaching ever again.

My father was a deeply wounded man.

Around sundown each day, I felt the dread of night looming ahead. There was no escaping the tornado coming toward us, but all we could do was hunker down and hope it didn't do too much damage.

First, there was the prayer. Every evening after the house was perfectly clean, dinner ready and waiting, Mom's hair and makeup freshened up for Dad's return from the day, I'd hear her yelling, "Jimmy, Sheri, get downstairs before your father gets home. We have to pray!" There we were, the three of us, standing together and facing our two big front doors. Mom would spread oil all over the doorway, anointing it as we would pray and ask God to keep out all the evil spirits that Dad was about to bring home from the bar. (You can only imagine what kind of images conjured up in our brains.) We begged God to let him be in a good mood, but it never seemed that He was listening or that we prayed hard enough.

After work, Dad would hang out for a few hours at a local bar called the Barru before heading home. He drank hard alcohol, mostly vodka, except on Saturdays when he would drink a few beers. How much he drank on Sundays depended on what sports team he was into, if they were winning or not, or how stressed he was about Monday coming too soon. But on weekdays, between 6 PM and 11 PM, Dad would show up at the house drunk, with the goal of becoming more drunk. The minute he would walk in the door, we could tell what kind of night it would be by the creepy look in his eyes. We did our best to stay out of the way–jump when he said jump, sit still and not move, and listen to the same song over and over. Anything and everything it would take to not upset him, which was difficult because he would always be searching for a reason to blow up.

Then my parents would begin to fight, which happened every night and lasted even into the early morning. Cussing, yelling, throwing items across the room, and slamming doors were the norm. Night after night, it would continue. Night after night, we would pray.

Talk about walking on eggshells. We became like professional dancers on those eggshells. In the evenings, Dad would turn his music up so loud that our neighbors thought we were having parties every night.

When my brother and I were in elementary school and my parents couldn't get a sitter on a Friday or Saturday night, they would take us with them to a jazz club on Highway 101 in Santa Monica, where my dad would play his trumpet. When we'd arrive around 9 or 10 PM, there'd be a booth waiting for us at the front, facing the stage. It was VIP seating–or so we thought anyway–and when my dad walked into the packed club, we felt like celebrities. The waitress had a drink on the table before we'd even get there, and Dad wasted no time, grabbing his horn and jumping on the stage.

My father was an excellent trumpet player and quite an entertainer, especially with a few cocktails in him. Those were actually proud moments for my brother and me. He was really good and could work a crowd like no other. During those moments, life felt kind of normal, even exciting. Everyone seemed happy, and the dad that was on stage playing was the dad I loved and admired. I kept *that* dad in my mind. I would tell myself, *That man is who my father really is, not the other guy.*

My brother and I would try our hardest not to fall asleep at the club, but those were late nights. Dad was always the last one to come off the stage, with only one or two people left sitting at the bar. When the party was over, Mom would wake us up, and we'd have to walk out to the car. I definitely didn't like that part of the night. Around 1 or 2 AM, it was always cold, and I wished I had my pajamas and a blanket with me.

Quite often, Dad would come home after work and tell us we were going out to dinner. It was a way he could drink more, have his company pay for it, and tell himself that he was a good father and husband by taking us all out to dinner. We would eat like royalty, stuffing ourselves with crab legs and filet mignon, while he'd toss back about seven Rob Roys on an empty stomach. Then he would insist on driving us all home, refusing to even hear of my mother taking the wheel. She never challenged him.

I remember it like it was yesterday. Starting in my elementary school years, I prepared myself to be the co-pilot for the ride home. I would position myself in the middle of the back seat so I could have a clear view of the road ahead, watching carefully for any danger, thinking maybe I could get us home alive. Mom would quickly fall asleep after getting in the car and sleep the whole way home with no problem. I, on the other hand, would sit with my eyes glued to the road ahead of us as Dad raced down the freeway, swerving to the right and then to the left, all the way home. I remember peeling back my stiff fingers, gripped to the seat in front of me, as we pulled into the driveway. A deep sigh of relief would come, as I was not aware I'd been holding my breath. *We made it!* The adrenaline pumping through my body made it hard to go to sleep, even though it was almost midnight.

Sometimes on school nights, we went to bed before Dad even got home. On these nights, Dad would come home from the bar close to midnight, park in the driveway beneath my bedroom, and hold down the car horn for our quiet neighborhood to hear. In response, I would jump up out of bed, run down the two flights of stairs, dash outside as fast as I could, and try to bargain with him to stop. The lights from our neighbors' homes would begin to flicker on, and I would inwardly panic, fearing embarrassment. On those nights, he would want me to plead with him to come in like it was a game. I would do it. Anything to get him to stop, to get him inside and me back to bed. Though I was just a little girl, I would have to help him out of the car, guide him up the stairs, almost carrying him into the house. I felt so ashamed. *What would the neighbors think?*

Mornings always came too soon after nights like these. I would feel Mom shaking me, "Sheri, get up!! You are going to be late for school!"

Late? I had just fallen back asleep.

Every morning, I had an emotional hangover–feeling achy and drained from the adrenaline rush of the evening before, combined with a lack of sleep. Though the previous night usually felt like World War I, the next morning, Dad would say "Good morning!" with a smile, and we would all carry on as though nothing had happened. When I arrived at school, I'd act like all was well and beautiful in the world, though inwardly I felt confused, scared, and terribly isolated. At an early age, I learned the useful skill of compartmentalization. I learned how to wear a mask.

This crazy and confusing cycle continued throughout my entire childhood.

My father made frequent trips to my room at night, while my mother was asleep. I would be woken up by the creak of my bedroom door as it opened, and the piercing shaft of the hall light, hitting me right in the face. Dad would quietly shut the door behind him, walk towards my bed, push me over just a little, and then roll his 200-pound body on top of mine.

The stench of alcohol and cigarettes was always overwhelming; his heavy body squishing into me and pressing all his drunkenness into my small frame. Dad would tell me that I was the only one who understood him and the only one who loved him, using a quiet, soft voice and becoming, at times, almost weepy with vulnerability. He would talk about whatever was on his mind, however long he wanted to talk.

I would lay still in the dark, taking in shallow breaths with my eyes wide open and my body frozen beneath him. I was scared to death to upset him, and yet in those moments, I experienced a different person than the dad I knew who went into rages. This was a father who felt human; one I felt sorry for. His countenance changed. He actually opened up and shared what was bothering him. He told me his life was hard, and he was a victim. He was not appreciated or treated fairly by Mom or his boss.

As a child, I interpreted these tense moments the best I could, which was that my dad was hurting, and I needed to help him. I would try to say smart things and show compassion, offering suggestions and encouragement.

"We appreciate you, Dad! We do," I would whisper, hoping to make him feel better so that he would just leave my room, and there would be no more fighting.

"We love you . . . . and God loves you. And really, Dad, isn't that the most important thing?"

This worked–temporarily. He would quiet down and leave my room just as he came. But after one of these nights, Dad would not speak to me or even look at me for a week or more.

Adding insult to injury, he'd lump me into fighting with Mom, cursing and accusing *all* of us at the same time, screaming, "YOU PEOPLE . . . !"

You said you trusted me and that I was special, different. Am I a part of the "you" in YOU PEOPLE? I would think.

I was baffled–and devastated. Though what my dad was doing was twisted and wrong, it still felt like a genuine connection to me. But he seemed to easily forget what we had shared, flying into rages again and again. As a result, I learned to second-guess my reality and to question my own feelings and intuition.

Between the ages of 8 and 13, my father visited my room this way, without my mother ever having a clue. The truth is, she was trying to hold on to her own sanity. To feel like she had some sense of control, Mom obsessively cleaned the house every day and poured herself into the church we attended. Still, she was always on the brink of a total meltdown, which happened frequently. When she did lose it, she would yell and cry, telling me she wanted to die and would explain to me the ways she thought she could do it. She wanted it over.

What was I to do with that information as a kid? *Jimmy and I must not be worth staying for, I would think.* And then, the scarier thought: *What would happen to us kids if Mom was gone? She's the sober one.*

My brother Jimmy was a very funny kid, and he loved to make me laugh. In the evenings, when my parents' fighting would get out of control, I would go into his room and get into bed with him to feel safe. We would lay there together for what seemed like forever, praying for the madness to stop while listening to my mother's screams and my father's profanity. As a young boy, Jimmy would sometimes jump out of bed in the middle of the night, go to where my parents were fighting, and stand between them. He would threaten my father, trying to protect my mother.

In response, Dad would just laugh at him and say a few words, trying to intimidate him. When Jimmy refused to back down, it actually seemed to get Dad's attention, and the fighting would simmer down a bit. I, on the other hand, would use the gentler approach of trying to counsel and reason with my parents to stop their fighting, and sometimes it worked.

My brother and I were in a war together, fellow soldiers in a daily battle. We were also each other's comfort and comic relief. However, every couple of weeks or so, when the tension would peak or Jimmy would get bored, he would come looking for me, and this never ended well.

"Sheri…where are you?" I'd hear him calling my name, footsteps pounding up the stairs to my room.

Panicked, I'd pray, "*Please, God, help me.*"

Jimmy loved to wrestle, and I did too, but I knew it was only a matter of time before I would get hurt. I'd hear him running up the stairs, calling my name. If I had enough time to escape, I would run and lock myself in the bathroom for however long it took for him to go away, or I would try nicely to tell him I didn't feel good. But that only added to his determination to mess with me. Inevitably, when we'd be playing, something would trigger him, and he would go into a rage.

Years later Jimmy explained to me what would happen: something would trigger him and everything in sight would turn red, he would lose control and become completely unaware that he was beating me. These episodes were something I feared but somehow accepted. My brother was put in a position he should have never had to be in as a child; the place of protector and husband to my mom and a parent to both mom and dad. Something had to give. All that built-up tension, rage, and frustration would have to go somewhere, and unfortunately, that somewhere was someone, and that someone was me. The way I learned to survive in my family–in Crazytown–was to make sure I didn't burden my parents with anything and learn to be whatever it was that I thought they needed: parent, counselor, confidant, and the one to walk them away from jumping off the cliff.

Stay at the helm! Steer the ship, and keep watch!

It was simply survival.

Chapter 2
The Prophet

Yehovah Tsebaoth, The LORD of Hosts

"Thus says the LORD, the King of Israel and his Redeemer, the LORD of hosts: 'I am the first and I am the last; besides me there is no god.'"

—Isaiah 44:6. ESV

El De'ot, God of Knowledge

"Boast no more so very proudly, Do not let arrogance come out of your mouth; For the LORD is a God of knowledge, And with Him actions are weighed."

—1 Samuel 2:3 NASB

When I was five years old, my mom started attending a church in Los Angeles called The Church of the Living Word. This church was founded by John Robert Stevens, a man who was thought by its members to be a prophet. In 1948, Stevens had become an ordained minister with the Assemblies of God denomination. In 1950, they removed him because of doctrinal differences, so he started his own church. He claimed to have had four different encounters with God, and in those encounters, God told him that he was *the anointed one*, a prophet sent by God. He was *the Apostle*.

My mother was a prime target to fall into this movement. She longed for connection and purpose, but I think she wanted someone to tell her what to do and how to think because life was just too much for her. After she found The Church of the Living Word–or "the Walk" as it was also known–we began to spend four days a week and many long hours sitting in church. Everyone talked about John Robert Stevens: the prophet, the man of God. "John, John, John," was all I heard. John was charismatic, loud, and powerful, and his congregants treated everything he said like gold. When he spoke, they were like baby birds sitting with their mouths hanging open, waiting to be fed by the only one whom they believed could feed them. People were always hoping he would simply walk by them or look at them–even just a glance would change their whole day. To be touched by him, or better yet spoken to by him, was the ultimate honor. Many times, during a church service, people would wait hours for him to actually show up. It didn't matter to him that people were waiting, and that church started at 5 pm; he often wouldn't arrive until 9 or 10 PM. It didn't matter to our parents that it was a school night, or that my brother and I had homework to finish. What mattered was that we waited for the Apostle.

Great excitement would fill the church when we'd finally hear, "The van is here! He's here!" The big moment everyone was waiting for had arrived. John always had an entourage of people surrounding him–including bodyguards–like he was a famous rock star or even the President of the United States. He would take his time, sitting in his fancy van with his chosen ones, until he was good and ready to come in. When he decided it was time to enter the church, the people would clear to the sides, making a path for him to enter. There was always a buzz in the air, and great anticipation to hear the so-called new revelation the prophet was going to give.

According to John, God was doing a new thing. He–the prophet– and we–God's Kingdom people–were the only ones in the entire universe who were privy to this heavenly knowledge. Much of the time, his preaching didn't make any sense. But what did I know? I was only a kid. His followers held onto every word, believing they came directly from the throne room of heaven. After all, in their eyes, he was *the* man of God. I didn't know then, but I know now: he was a drunk. His bloodshot eyes behind his bifocals were as big as saucers. *Are those the eyes of a prophet?* I secretly wondered.

At The Church of the Living Word, we were taught not to think for ourselves, and that emotions and self-awareness were of the devil. We were taught to submit to the appointed elders and shepherds because they were the ones who could hear the will of God for our lives, including how parents should raise their children. I remember hurting my knee as a young child, and my mom taking me to a Thursday morning service to get prayer from John Robert Stevens. We waited for a couple hours before I heard my name called to go forward. I was scared. He would stare into people with his big saucer eyes, "tune in to their spirits," and then speak what he heard from God. His big, weighty eyes pierced into my soul and saw everything in me . . . or at least that is what I was told. He could see things I didn't even know were there, as well as those things I did know: the little white lie I told my mom or the fight I got into with my brother.

I stood there nervously waiting. After pressing his hand down on my head, he told my mom to take me to a chiropractor and that I had a spirit of lust on me. Then, he directed the church to join him in rebuking the spirit of lust. Hundreds of congregants were loudly shouting at me, only eight years old at the time. *What is lust? I have lust?* I thought. When we got in the car to make the long trip home that afternoon, I asked my mom what lust was.

She was always thinking of a million other things, and I never knew how she would react to my questions. She quickly blurted out, "It's a perversion. Oh gosh, I need to go and pick up some chicken and vegetables tonight and drop by Sears and get . . ."

I interrupted her ramblings, "What is a perversion?"

Preoccupied, she quickly answered, "Oh, it's like sexy, you know sexual lusty stuff. Your father has lust," and she went on with her list of what she had to do.

I felt my face go hot with shame. My dirtiness was announced on a microphone and the whole church knew. I felt marked that day. *I am bad and I have lust.* I went home and cried out to God to help me. I did not feel like I had what my mom explained to me, but I knew I must because the prophet said I did.

In The Church of the Living Word, it was very common for children to be sent away from their families to other affiliated churches in the country. There were churches in Oregon and Hawaii and a community called Shiloh in Iowa, which was essentially a big farm where they'd put people–including children–to work. It didn't matter if a child was in school. If this was the "leading and direction" given, he or she would have to drop out of class and go. No one considered how sending a child away could put them in danger or traumatize them. It was simply received as the will of God. As children, we knew that at any given time, John Roberts Stevens had the power to send us away from our families. And we knew our parents wouldn't resist.

I grew up afraid of God but wanted so badly to know Him, as most of us did. The Walk was filled with people with sincere and devoted hearts who wanted to please God, but our understanding of knowing Him meant being approved by church leaders and the prophet himself. I was aware that the eyes of many "shepherds" were on me all the time. I was desperately afraid of being disobedient. The church was a huge part of who I was, and the people were my family. Disobedience meant I would be cut off, no longer part of God's people: disconnected, excommunicated and shamed. I lived with constant inner strife and continuously examined myself wondering, *Could I be a betrayer like Judas?* I didn't trust myself to know. *Do I have a seducing Jezebel spirit?* That was another term you didn't want to be labeled with. It's no wonder I was afraid.

At the church, we lived in constant fear, but we were also taught that we had a special power. We engaged in a practice called "throwing rocks" at God during which we would move our bodies as if we were hurtling boulders, demanding God to act. We also spent hours cursing and damning others who had supposedly rebelled, making death decrees and praying judgment on them. It was an adrenaline rush being in those meetings, yelling our heads off at God for a couple hours or more. We would use our whole body to intercede: stomping, clapping, yelling, and singing. "We won't look back like Lot's wife, remember not the past," were the lyrics to a popular song in the church that sounded like it came right out of a Broadway musical. We were even taught that our thumbs had authority, and as we cast our judgments, we would have our thumbs up for an increase of power.

Those who left the Walk or betrayed leadership in some way were considered Nephilim and deserving of judgment. Nephilim were the beings written about in Genesis 6 in the Bible, during the time of Noah. Meaning "fallen ones," they were part human, part supernatural offspring of fallen angels having sex with the daughters of men. The way it was taught to us, Nephilim were evil giants, destructive forces who still lived on earth and had even attended our church. I will never forget when we were told to pray for the destruction of John's ex-wife, who was now considered a Nephilim. The truth was the apostle had left her after almost thirty years of marriage for his much younger secretary, Marilyn.

This was the beginning of what the church called a "Kingdom marriage," which was the spiritual term used when someone in leadership wanted to divorce their spouse to be with someone else. This new thing the "Spirit" was leading became quite popular actually, and the church accepted divorce into its theology as being for the Kingdom of God. The church also believed in arranged marriages, including young girls just out of high school marrying older men. The abortions of babies were mandated by leadership as well. To this day, I have no idea what the motive behind this was, other than pure evil.

After ten years of being in this cult, I entered high school. Life was becoming quite confusing, and I found my anxiety spiraling out of control. There were two totally different lives competing within me, and I was trying to successfully survive in both worlds. On the one hand, I was trying to succeed in the church, which gave me my identity and purpose, and on the other hand, I was trying to succeed in high school, with all its social and academic pressures. I found drama and acting and did well at it, which allowed me to be someone else for a while each day. It also helped to keep people from knowing the real me, while being likable enough to stay safe. I learned to make people laugh and was even voted class clown. But on the inside, I was still trapped in my cult upbringing and church. One of the main teachings of John Roberts Stevens was not to have any "bonds" with people outside the church. I had friends, grandmothers, aunts, and cousins that I loved, but with whom I couldn't have a "bond." I remember wondering, *How do I survive in this world and at the same time be careful not to bond? What exactly is a bond anyway, so I can watch for it if it happens?*

Sometimes during a church service, we would even take time to do some "bond breaking." We were told to put our hands on the back of our heads, visualizing the person with whom we possibly had a bond. With a few hundred others, we'd say the person's name out loud and curse the bond. After that, we would shake our hands, as if to shake off water. I'll never forget when the prophet told everyone to go to a certain member of the church to get our hair cut. A couple weeks later, there was an announcement that this hair stylist had been ex-communicated from the "body", and all who had their hair done by him needed to line up at the front of the church so the elders could break the bond that was created by his hands touching our heads. I don't know what happened. Maybe he gave the prophet a bad haircut, but whatever it was, it wasn't good.

In the depths of his alcohol addiction, my dad was ironically ordained to be an elder in our local branch of the Walk. I would almost die of shame when he came to church drunk, which happened to be every time. I was hypervigilant, watching every move, dreading when he would get up out of his seat with a burning desire to give a "prophetic word." His drunken, spiritual babble was horribly embarrassing. He had started going to the church because he had joined us at a few of the weekend parties put on by the church family, typically flowing with alcohol. Mom had been asking the members to be praying for dad to join the church for years, so they were praising God that their prayers

were being answered. He was showing up! To drink and play pool, but showing up!

The leaders in the church even made my dad an elder, probably because he impressed them with a trivia fact or two. My dad was book smart: a walking encyclopedia, no exaggeration. Still, he acted like a drunk in church. He was known for the little jingle he'd sing every time he'd be at the pulpit, "Accentuate the positive, eliminate the negative." Every time he got up to speak, I wanted to run and hide. I would hold my breath, dreading what he would say. I guess people weren't as aware and affected as I was. It was all so crazy that he fit in just fine.

The impact of being a part of The Church of the Living Word didn't end when we left the physical building. I remember when the prophet told everyone in the church to commit their spirits to Marilyn, his former secretary who had become his wife because she knew best how to channel our prayers more effectively. The "Channeling Hour" was a part of a practice we were mandated to do known as "Combat Communication" which would happen around 3:00 AM throughout the week. Marilyn and John were receiving "messages from God" each night that needed to be communicated to the church, and Combat Communication operated as a phone tree to alert all The Living Word churches of what was happening in the Spirit. Each night, we were to have our pen and paper ready in case the call came through. In our group, my brother got the call first. He would call me from his bedroom downstairs to share the breaking Kingdom news or mandated prayer direction during Channeling Hour. I would call the next person and it would go on from there. Typically, the message would be a combination of one-liners that rarely made any sense. But we were taught to treat them like codes that we dare not question. After writing out the message, we'd repeat it back to make sure we got it right before calling and reporting to the next person on the phone tree. That continued for years, and as a teenager, I was woken up almost every night to hear an urgent message for the church, most likely shared by the leader in a state of drunkenness.

When I was about fifteen and had been in The Church of the Living Word for ten years, I wanted the prophet to see that I was someone

who would be a great fit in his inner circle, a true worshiper. Nothing was as important as being recognized as a true and pure follower of John Robert Stevens–not school, a career, not even family. He would be standing on the stage looking out at all the people as they stood worshiping and praying. I would pray harder and sing louder, hoping he would notice me in the crowd, and see that I was a true and trusted follower. I'd think to myself, *He is a prophet, so he must see my heart.* I thought if he would notice me, then I would be special. But week after week, he didn't see me. Why were others chosen and not me? The shame of not being enough combined with my alcoholic home created a huge identity crisis that tormented me beyond words. If my dad didn't see me, my mom didn't see me, and John Robert Stevens didn't see me, I must not be worth seeing.

The summer before my sophomore year, I met a boy and had my first kiss. I was terrified that I had committed rebellion. The night of the kiss, I walked back to the beach house I was staying at, praying the whole way home. My friend who had invited me to go with her and her family was already asleep in the bed across the room from mine. I felt I had betrayed God with that kiss and feared I had broken my connection with Him. The minute I laid down; I started the process of breaking bonds with the boy. I went into intense prayer, asking God for forgiveness while moving my hands in front of my face, like I was opening curtains, reaching up towards Heaven, trying to regain my connection with God. About ten minutes into doing this, I heard my friend say, "What are you doing?" I almost died. I had no idea she had been watching me, and I nervously made up some silly excuse and quickly steered her away from asking any more questions by talking about something else. Still, she was totally freaked out, seeing me perform what must have looked like voodoo. But that was the real me at the time, the "church me." Sadly, our friendship changed that night, and we grew apart. It became obvious that she shared with her friends what she had seen me doing. That group of girls treated me like I was strange after that. Honestly, I don't blame them. I was strange.

Chapter 3
Good Father

Yahweh Mekkacishkhem,
The LORD your Sanctifier

"Consecrate yourselves and be holy, because I am the LORD your God. Keep my decrees and follow them. I am the LORD, who makes you holy."

—Leviticus 20:7-8

Elohim Emet, True God

"But the LORD is the true God; He is the living God, the eternal King . . ."

—Jeremiah 10:10

Tortured with shame and anxiety and living a double life, I finally hit a wall at age 17. I had faith in God but was confused and afraid of Him. Not only that, but I had zero respect for both my parents. Frustrated and desperate for something to make sense, I decided to sell my car and go as

far away from home as possible–at least temporarily. I ended up in New York City, where some friends from the church had opened their home for me to stay for as long as I wanted.

New York had always fascinated me, but I wasn't going there to sightsee. This trip felt like life or death to me. I told God that if He was real, He needed to show up. I decided that I wasn't going to leave New York until He revealed Himself. If He didn't show up, I would have my answer and would go my own way.

Deep in my heart, however, I knew God was real. Up to that point, I had pursued Him the best way I knew how. But why all the pain and suffering?

Why all the unanswered prayers for my dad?

Why does he continue to be an alcoholic and abusive to our family?

Why is my mother so unstable and depressed when all we do is pray?

If we're Kingdom people, chosen to be under the guidance of the prophet and obedient and faithful to his teachings, then why are we all such a mess?

All these questions led me to this moment: alone in a tiny apartment in New York City, waiting for God to speak. For days on end, I did nothing but wait for an answer and read my Bible. If you could picture someone tapping their foot while waiting, irritated and impatient, for someone to do something, that was me. I spent most of my time on or around the couch. I lied down, I sat up, and I kneeled down. I read, and I waited.

Despite my impatience, I did feel some peace being there because I was away from all the drama at home. Still, my prayers were not being answered in the way I expected. I waited to hear God's audible voice, a thunderclap from heaven, or *anything* to give me the answers I desperately needed.

And then, after about three weeks of waiting, something radical happened.

I was reading the book of Galatians when suddenly, the words went from just words on a page to being completely alive, almost vibrating with life and meaning.

"I have been crucified with Christ; and it is no longer I who live, but Christ lives in me; and the life which I now live in the flesh I live by faith in the Son of God, who loved me and gave Himself up for me."

—Galatians 2:20 NASB

I felt like I had left a room of total darkness, from not even being able to see my hands in front of my face to entering a brightly-lit room where I could see every detail illuminated. In an instant, I began to see and understand what Jesus did for me on the cross.

Jesus did what?

Though I had heard the gospel before, though I knew who Jesus was, I never understood what He actually paid for. I never understood what His death and resurrection really meant for me, for my life.

Love walked into the room that day and changed everything.

I started laughing as I continued reading because I felt as if the words were literally jumping off the pages. At that moment, I realized that it wasn't really about me. It was all about Jesus and what He did for me. I could never be good enough or smart enough. I could never be sinless and perfect.

I kept asking God, *"The cross took care of everything? Really? Jesus paid for* all *my sins?"*

Yes. I knew the answer. *Yes.*

This radical revelation of grace tore away at the lie that I had to be perfect. It was the first time I had ever really felt free.

But it was more than the revelation that opened my eyes. It was my Heavenly Father coming to rescue His prodigal daughter. It felt like He had placed the robe around me and the ring on my finger saying, *"I am your father. I love you. I see you. I know who you are. You are my beautiful child."*

I remember walking around the room, breaking out in a dance with my hands up to the heavens, laughing and crying at the same time. I continued to read my Bible throughout the night and felt the words releasing shackles as if chains had been wrapped around my

mind. I was amazed and touched (I think it is a stronger word than touched). The God of the universe saw me and was speaking to me intimately.

I was born again.

As I was celebrating that evening, I heard a small voice: a gentle whisper inside my heart saying that John Robert Stevens was not a prophet. Of course, I had already had a sense that things weren't what I thought they were in the Living Word Church. The Holy Spirit was quick in wanting to reveal the truth to me. But in many ways, I was still programmed by fear. I had no context to believe that the teaching of the Walk was not of God. I thought Satan was attacking me. I was also scared to death to be a Nephilim, one of the fallen ones who brought division to the church.

So I began praying, rejecting any thoughts that told me that John Roberts Stevens was a fraud. I actually went into intense intercession, fighting the devil and resisting the seeds I believed he had planted in my mind. I believed he was trying to use me to bring destruction to the prophet, and I begged God to send the devil away from me, repenting for having a thought like that. I went into what we called "hand-to-hand combat," which was how I had been taught to fight the devil. Using my arms like a sword and with my thumbs up, I rebuked any spirits that would want to destroy the prophet, commanding them to die.

After a few hours of this, I felt the gentleness of God, my Father, tenderly say, *"It's okay, Sheri. It's okay."* He simply lifted that burden off of me, waiting for another time to give me a full revelation of what was really going on. Now, I know that He was protecting me, understanding how fragile I was. However, that little seed of truth that something wasn't right with the church and the prophet planted itself in the back of my mind.

I returned home a couple weeks later a changed person. I was eager to share the gospel and lay hands on the sick, fully believing they would be healed just like the Bible says. Every chance I had, I shared with people, prayed for them, and told them about the God I had encountered. I was on fire, and I wanted everyone to have what I had.

But all that didn't work out like I hoped it would.

One Sunday after church, I was told by one of the leaders that I was being called into an important meeting. They brought me into the meeting room in the back of the church, where I nervously faced the elders, my brother being one of them. It was about 100 degrees that day, and I remember the room was stiflingly hot and completely silent as I entered. The elders looked at me like I was busted for something I did wrong. It became quickly apparent to me that they had all met beforehand to discuss me, the "issue" at hand. I took my seat at the front, facing around 20 men. I remember thinking, *This is serious. What in the world could this be about?*

I started doing an inventory in my head, going over everything I had done wrong in the last few years. After what felt like an hour of silence, but was only a few minutes, one of the elders spoke up for the group.

"You need to be quiet."

"I'm sorry, Can you repeat that?" I said nervously. *Did he just say to be quiet? I haven't said a word since I walked in.*

"You need to be quiet," he said again, this time with more force.

I sat there with a confused look on my face.

Seeing that I wasn't getting it, another elder spoke up. "Let me put it this way Sheri: An empty wagon makes a lot of noise."

"Huh? What does that mean?" I responded.

Finally, another elder interpreted it all clearly. He told me that everything I had been sharing recently had no value. Simply put, they wanted me to shut up.

My ears felt hot with shame. I sat there and tried not to look uncomfortable or as awkward as this situation was but smiled and put on an act. *It's cool. It's all good,* I tried to convey. But the truth is, I was humiliated.

The feeling was as if you'd received an invitation to a birthday party and you were really excited to be invited. But after you arrive, you find out the invitation wasn't for you. To make it worse, the birthday girl asks why you are there in front of everybody. Embarrassed and fumbling to find something to say while trying to act like it's no big deal, you make up some excuse as your neck and face flush red. What was I to do? They were the elders. I submitted out of fear. I wanted to please God and remain 100% loyal to the church.

However, what happened in New York could never be taken from me. I was with Jesus.

Still, the words "An empty wagon makes a lot of noise" replayed in my mind over and over for many years to come.

An empty wagon . . . . an empty wagon makes a lot of noise.

I will never forget that day, nor those words or the look in the man's eyes as he spoke them slowly and directly to me: the words that would try and silence me for a lifetime. Once we got home that night, my brother didn't say anything to me about the meeting. It did feel awkward, but church business was church business, and we both knew that. He was an elder and had an important role in the church. The main thing for both the elders and the members was to submit and not ask questions. We would never think to challenge or disagree with what leadership was doing or saying, even when it came to family members.

About a year later, just before I turned 19, John Roberts Stevens died. Our leader, the Apostle, *the* man of God was dead. The whole church was shocked.

The church sent out a Combat Communication demanding an emergency nationwide prayer vigil calling us into three days of 24-hour prayer and intercession. People flooded into the Los Angeles church from all over the country to pray. The church as a whole coming together like this for feasts and times of prayer was nothing unusual, as we would be called into these intense meetings from time to time. My understanding was that this was going to be a time for all the Living Word churches to come together and comfort each other, grieve, and receive direction for what was next. I believed we would answer the big question: *Who will carry the prophet's mantle now that he is in Heaven?*

The church was packed, with standing room only for the entire three days. I remember the chaos, shoulder-to-shoulder sweaty bodies, and people yelling out to God in continuous, violent intercession. But on the third night, the last day of the vigil, I heard something differ-ent. The direction coming from the elders was now to pray for resur-

rection. The people were crying out to God, demanding that He raise John Robert Stevens from the dead on the third day because *he was the Christ*.

Did I just hear what I think I heard? Do they believe John will rise from the dead because he is Christ, as in Jesus Christ?

I couldn't believe what I was hearing. "John Robert Stevens is the Christ!" I heard, again and again. They believed he would be raised from the dead on the third day, just like Jesus was, and time was running out.

Suddenly everything felt like it was going in slow motion. I stood towards the front of the church, squishing myself into the crowd to get as close to all the action as possible, listening carefully to what the people were demanding of God. Through the pressure of the crowd and all the noise, I could hear the people clearly yelling, "John Robert Stevens is the Christ!"

I looked out over the sea of people, searching through the crowd for my brother's eyes. I wanted to know if he was hearing what I was, but I couldn't find him. It was at that moment that I began to understand what God was trying to tell me in New York. *This is really happening. What does this mean for me? For my family and friends?*

Question after question tumbled through my mind. But the loudest, clearest one was *What should I do?*

It was devastating, like the ground that we had stood on for so long, had been hit by an earthquake, and we were left standing on a giant split in the earth beneath us.

I believe now that if I hadn't been born again a year before, I wouldn't have seen it so clearly, nor have handled it as well as I did.

When it was obvious that the prophet was not going to be raised from the dead–I later heard that they kept his body and waited for almost two weeks–his wife Marilyn became very angry and blamed the entire congregation. According to her, our prayers did not have enough power to bring him back. It was our fault that he didn't rise.

Later on, it became clear that she and another leader in the church were having an affair the whole time John was sick. Gary was a married man with one child and one on the way, and right after John died, he announced his divorce to the congregation. He and Marilyn were getting married. It was, as I mentioned earlier, "a kingdom marriage."

After the last night of the third day, my mom, my brother, and I all came together to discuss what was happening. It was a gift to process this giant wrecking ball together. Other families were divided, causing devastation for many of my friends. People were cut off from each other immediately depending on who was staying and who was leaving what was now being called what it was: a cult. As the days went by, my brother learned more from a few of the senior leaders, revealing deeper and deeper layers of the twisted truth.

I was 19 years old when we left the cult. My brother was 21.

Mom and Dad left, too. Because my brother was a highly respected elder in the cult and played a parent role to both of them, what he said carried a lot of weight in the decision for them to leave. The church was just an ego feed for dad, and he'd only been going for a few years at that point. As for me, I didn't need additional reassurance. I knew what I was hearing and becoming aware of on my own but was grateful we were in this together.

When it came down to it, leaving The Walk was actually a painful tearing away from people we loved. Since I was five years old, we had developed relationships with people at the church. They were my family: the people with whom I was allowed to "bond." Brokenhearted, knowing full well what this would mean for us, we had to go. We were cut from the church and its members completely and are now considered dead to them. Not only dead but enemies, demonic forces, Nephilim; we were everything I never wanted to be. We were traitors. I was left with one question: *Has anything I have believed and built my life and relationships on been true?*

I began the journey of finding out.

Chapter 4
Released but Brainwashed

El Rakhum, Merciful God

"For the LORD your God is a merciful God; he will not abandon you or destroy you or forget the solemn covenant he made with your ancestors."

—Deuteronomy 4:31 NLT

El Nasah, God of Forgiveness

"[O] LORD our God, you answered them; you were to Israel a forgiving God, though you punished their misdeeds."

—Psalm 99:8

"You forgave the iniquity of your people and covered all their sins. You set aside all your wrath and turned from your fierce anger."

—Psalm 85:2-3

When I left the cult in 1983, I found myself free of many things, including a ridiculously tight church schedule, religion, and performance anxiety. But I wasn't completely free. I was looking for love and security and found myself in a relationship with a guy exactly like my father–an abusive alcoholic. This guy, however, took it a step further and added in whatever high was available at the time: smoking pot, using meth and snorting cocaine.

At 19 years old, only a couple months after leaving the cult, I decided to marry him. We were sleeping together, so I thought this was the best solution to get me out of sin. Plus, choosing to get married felt like emancipation. In the cult, we weren't allowed to make decisions without first submitting to the elders. They were the authority God had placed over everyone, and the restrictions on women were even worse. I kept reminding myself, *I am free. I'm not under the cult anymore. Free to make my own decisions.* Marriage felt like a way for me to claim this newfound freedom. I had to take control of my own life, to make my own decisions.

But it would soon become clear that it would take a long time to actually heal my brainwashed mind, and marriage to this man would hardly help.

After my boyfriend and I were married in a quick, low-budget wedding, we boarded a plane that same day and moved to a place I had never been before, Steamboat Springs, Colorado, where my new husband had already been working as a roofer. After the ceremony, I said goodbye to my family and the few friends I had and left Los Angeles. That first night of marriage, he took me to his favorite watering hole in town, a dark, smoky bar filled only with men drinking and playing pool. It was in those first hours of marriage that I knew, as I watched my new husband play pool for hours while I sat next to a passed-out drunk who kept falling on me, that I had just made a huge mistake.

After only a couple months, I became pregnant. I was excited, but my husband treated me like I had done something wrong, and I'd better deal with it. My cult mentality told me that I was to submit and that God's will was to do what my husband told me to do, which was to get an abortion. Broken-hearted by what he commanded, I didn't know I had a choice or a voice. I had been programmed my entire life, through both the teaching of the cult and by my role models, that men had surpassing authority. No matter how terrible the decisions they made were, you were to submit. That was what was most pleasing to God. In the cult, my mom would approach the elders about my father's abusiveness towards her, but they continually told her she had to submit to him. They took scripture out of context all the time; she was to win him over *with a meek and quiet spirit.*

I called my mom and told her I was pregnant and what my husband told me I had to do. I remember that it was a tender moment between us. She cried with me on the phone and connected with my pain, which was unusual for her and deeply comforting to me. Her tears were because of what she was about to say. "You have to do this. There is nothing else you can do. This is so sad, Sheri. I'm sorry." She was a mother with no voice, who had allowed herself to be abused for the last 27 years. What else could she say to her daughter at that moment?

Full of shame, with no support and with marching orders from my husband, I had to figure out how to get an abortion. Where was I supposed to look in this new town with a tiny population? The yellow pages? Call 411? I didn't know a soul, but I had a job in a local real estate office in town and had become somewhat friendly with the receptionist there. Nervously, I told her that I was pregnant and asked her if she knew where I could go. She told me there was only one doctor in town who would do it. Pulling me into the bathroom, she quietly gave me his name and number and scribbled discreetly on a piece of paper. I called and made the appointment the next day.

During this time, I felt lost, like an empty shell, disconnected from myself and others. It felt like so many parts of me were broken, and it was impossible to connect during the short conversations I had with others and during interactions with my husband. Hurt and confusion were tucked away somewhere deep inside me, but for me, the abortion was just another brutal situation to stuff down. I really didn't have any expectations of my husband, and my only expectation for myself was to be the best wife I could possibly be. My husband cared about three things: partying, sex, and my cooking. He spent most of his time outside of the house, drinking, using, and womanizing–which I knew about.

One afternoon, I had to go to the office where my husband worked to pick up his paycheck, and for some reason, probably because I had no one to talk to, I shared with the lady at the front desk that I was pregnant and having an abortion. Startled by what I said, she quickly responded "Why are you having an abortion?"

"Because my husband said I have to."

She looked at me like I was out of my mind. "It is your body and your baby. You don't have to do anything you don't want to do. No one can tell you what to do with your own body. Do you want to have an abortion?"

"No," I responded.

She said it again. "It's your body, your life, and your baby. You don't have to do this!"

She was so strong and confident; it blew me away. But what she was saying was like hearing a foreign language. I kept thinking to myself, *There is no way I would ever think of not submitting to what I was told to do, especially by my husband. That could not be God's will.* As much as I was moved by her words and strength, I could not accept what she told me.

As I walked to the doctor's office to have the abortion, I felt heartsick and shaky. After it was over, my husband agreed to pick me up only because the doctor said I couldn't walk home. Once again, I disassociated to survive. Other than briefly acknowledging that it was finished, my husband didn't speak of the abortion at all. I have never felt as alone as I did that night.

I became pregnant again about five months later, but this time, something powerful was rising up within me. Like some new woman, I heard a voice say, *Enough you tyrant!*

Enough.

One evening, when my husband came home from work, I simply told him, "I am pregnant, and I am having this baby." For the first time ever, I didn't care if he was mad at me. I wasn't scared to be treated badly.

I felt 100% sure of my decision, and I only wanted to protect this child. I thanked God for this blessing and that I was given another chance after what I had done.

A couple days later, my husband came home and told me we were moving back to California. We were going to San Diego, and we would be living with an old high school buddy of his, whom I'd never met and knew nothing about. The good news, however, was that we were going back to California. We packed up the car with all of our belongings and headed to San Diego. It had been a long, cold, and lonely winter in Colorado, and driving west, I felt a little thrill, thinking about sunshine and the beach.

I was 20 years old, and my life was about to take another dramatic turn.

In San Diego, I found a job right away bagging groceries at Ralph's Grocery store close to where we were living in Point Loma. I worked with a few friendly girls around my age, who let me know right away they were Christians and showed an interest in getting to know me. After leaving the church, I was reluctant to open up to anybody who claimed to be Christian, but they seemed genuine. They would ask me questions about my life and my husband and even invited me to hang out, which I didn't feel ready to do. But still, I appreciated the offer. Their kindness helped me to open up, and I eventually shared a little bit about my difficult marriage, which I could tell concerned them. One of the girls suggested counseling and told me about a great guy she knew, a counselor at her church called Calvary Chapel. I thought about it for a few days, and then told her I would go. She scheduled an appointment for me to meet with him the following week.

I remember pulling up to the church where his office was and feeling nervous. This was the first church I had been to since leaving the cult, and I hadn't faced a "man of God" for a while. I was also aware that I was putting myself in a vulnerable position. To me, men had all the power, so what he would say about me and to me would not be taken lightly. Not to mention, we would be alone together in his office. I remember that I could tell he was feeling a little helpless, not able to get through to me. He asked me questions, and I smiled, giving short and simple answers. I was a bit like a Stepford wife. I knew what to say and how to answer, but I was disassociated, almost robotic.

He finally tried a different approach. "How about we try something. I'm going to give you a scenario and you tell me what you would do, okay?"

"Sure!" I responded pertly, smiling of course.

"What if I told you to meet me at midnight down at the docks in downtown San Diego. Would you go?"

"Yes!"

At the time, downtown San Diego was a pretty scary place to hang out at any time of the day, let alone midnight. A bit shocked, he continued, "Okay . . . There are no lights, it's pitch-black outside, and it's just you and me. What if I told you there were sharks in the water, but we are going in anyway? I want you to go in first, before me, and I will go in after you. Would you go?"

"Yes," I quickly responded.

He looked sad, defeated. "Why? Why would you do that? There are sharks in the water. You don't know me. It's dark, and it's the middle of the night. Why would you go?"

"Because you told me to," I responded. He stared at me for a few moments. He had no words, but I could tell he was both frustrated and compassionate. He asked if he could pray for me, and then sent me on my way. I guess my case was something he had never dealt with before and didn't know how to handle. I felt weird leaving his office. I had the feeling that I had done something wrong and felt embarrassed and confused. *What did I do?* I thought. I believed I had answered correctly. *I'm supposed to do what I am told, and God will protect me.* Right?

One day, when I was four months pregnant and at work, I started cramping. By that night, I began bleeding. I called my doctor, who told me to come to his office the next morning. After my exam, he said it was nothing to worry about. I had just had a sonogram a couple weeks before, and everything had looked perfectly normal. The bleeding was light but continued throughout the day. He didn't give me directions to stay off my feet or take it easy but assured me that this was normal and not to worry. Then, in the middle of the night, I was awakened by sharp pain and a bed full of blood. My husband took me to the emergency room, where I was diagnosed with a condition called placenta previa. The doctor explained what it was and that the baby had a 50% chance of surviving, but only if I could hold on to the pregnancy for at least another four months. I was told it was mandatory for me to be on total bed rest and would have to stay that way until the baby's lungs were mature enough for it to be born.

My husband did not want the baby and definitely did not want to care for me, so I decided to get to a place where I could stay in bed and have someone there to help me. I decided to move back in with my parents in Los Angeles. Although my father was drinking more than ever, my brother lived close by, and I was confident that he would be there for me too. I was just grateful I had somewhere to go.

After the long train ride up to LA, my bleeding increased to a new level, to the point that I ended up in the hospital that next day and remained there for a month. My doctor told me that if I could stay completely flat on my back, there was a chance that the placenta could actually move into the right position as the baby grew, which would cause the bleeding to stop and help carry the baby to full term. However, I would have to stay on my back in the hospital, taking it one day at a time.

The bleeding continued each day, and I had to have multiple blood transfusions throughout my stay. The doctors warned me that if the baby survived, there was a significant chance the baby could have brain damage because of the amount of blood loss. Despite everything I felt God's love and presence with me. Psalm 34:18 says that "[He] is near to the brokenhearted and saves those who are crushed in spirit." No matter what was going on with my body, I felt His peace.

My brother had a couple weeks off from work during that time, so he came every day to the hospital just to be with me. He'd get there right when visiting hours started and would be the last to leave at 10 PM each night. He brought me a book that was the first piece of Christian literature I had read after leaving the cult. Up to that point, I had only read the Bible and Living Word material, but Jim brought me *A Christian's*

Secret of a Happy Life written by Hannah Whitall Smith in the 1800s. Reading it was like drinking a cold glass of water and discovering that you are way thirstier than you realized. This book once again opened my eyes to a perfect loving Father God, the same One I had met when I was 17 in that apartment in New York City. This was a Father I could trust and trust my child with.

While I was in the hospital, a few people were praying for me who had also left the cult. They sent urgent messages through my mom, telling me this baby's life or death was up to me. They said that I had the power and authority to tell this situation to change. This way of thinking was familiar to me but definitely did not feel like the truth. In the cult, we told God what to do. We did not rest in the fact that He is a loving God, who is good. We didn't consider that God would know exactly what was needed in a situation. We just commanded what we wanted to happen. I loved this baby inside me. I was bonding with him and felt so much comfort having him with me. It felt like we were a team, holding on together through each day. But the continuous bleeding was a constant reminder that I had to surrender the outcome of what would happen.

After two weeks of being in the hospital, and only five-and-a-half months pregnant, my water broke. The doctors assumed I would be having the baby that day, but I surprised them and held on for another two weeks–never knowing what would come next. Continual bleeding, daily going in and out of intense premature labor for hours at a time, being rushed into the delivery room again and again. When it would stop, I would be brought back to my room where I'd wait for whatever was next. The constant poking and prodding in search of a vein that hadn't collapsed was becoming wearisome. I remember lying there alone, after eight attempts to find a vein and crying out loud, "Why hast thou forsaken me? Please God, help them find my vein!" I desperately wanted to hold on until the baby's lungs were mature enough for me to give birth. Every day I prayed the bleeding would stop, the placenta would move, and for the water sack to reseal itself and stop leaking. Every morning, I would hope that I could hold on one more day, waiting, trusting, and surrendering.

On November 1, 1984, I woke up with a different feeling in my body. I had complete peace, but the pain was at a level 10. I was in labor. After six hours of hard labor, my firstborn son was born at only six months, weighing one pound and two ounces. As I lay there in the delivery room looking over at my son, I was completely mesmerized by how beautiful and perfect his little body was. I couldn't believe I was looking at *my* child, the one who had been with me for the last six months. The one I fought for, and the one who fought for me. He lived only a couple of hours. I named him David, after King David because he was a fighter and stayed with me, until the end. He taught me a lot and brought me great comfort and love while I carried him. Despite the pain of this pregnancy, my relationship with my Father God had deepened tremendously. My heart opened up more to Him in these darkest of hours, and healing and restoration happened. His counsel and comfort felt tangible through the days and nights while both David and I were fighting for life. I was aware of something else happening; my mind was beginning to heal from some of the dysfunctional programming I had. Losing a child sounds like the opposite of a time of healing, but I was experiencing the presence of God. His kindness and tenderness were with me constantly as we were taken care of by a team of wonderful doctors and nurses, deeply invested in our lives. When it was time to leave after a month's stay, they all came to my room with tears and hugs and so much love for me and my baby. At the time, I was blown away. People really cared about me, and I could feel it was real. I had not seen my husband one time during that entire stay at the hospital, but I felt genuinely cared for by those God had put around me, and I knew that I was seen and held by God Himself.

I arrived back at my house in San Diego with a simple welcome, as though I had returned from work for the day. It was as if nothing had happened because nothing had happened to *him*. The world had totally stopped for me. My husband was a free man, unaffected and unaware. With my heart broken, belly empty, breasts filled with milk, and no child to nurse or hold in my arms, I knew no other way other than to keep living. I noticed how life strangely continued on for the world around me. My world, however, had been radically changed by the death of my child. And I had changed also. As my body was returning to normal, strength was rising up inside of me. I had been in the valley of death, and God had been with me there, every day and all through the night.

Soon after David's passing, my dad was charged with another D.U.I. This was number ten in his drinking career. At the time, the laws were a bit lax on drinking and driving, which hadn't helped the situation. But at 56 years old, with the cops standing at his car door, flashing a bright light into his eyes, my dad finally decided the party was over and that his last drink that night was indeed his last drink. One positive thing about my dad was that if he committed to something, which was rare, he would do it. I knew if he said he was done, he was done.

He was taken to jail, but this time, he chose to wait until they released him instead of telling mom to bail him out. He was willing to face the consequences, although he still got off pretty easily. He had to pay a fine and stay a few weekends in the local jail, which he was happy to do. He enjoyed the peace and quiet to read books and do his crossword puzzles and not being bothered by mom. He also went into a 30-day spin dry rehab and actually liked the program and enjoyed the fellowship of other alcoholics wanting to be sober. During his stay, my mom, brother, and I were asked to attend a couple family therapy sessions, and it was there that I began to understand that alcoholism is truly a disease. Reality dawned on me, or rather, it smacked me in the face. I was married to an alcoholic, a man just like my father. I had become my mother and was repeating the whole sick cycle that tried to kill me.

Immediately, I started going to 12-step meetings, Adult Children of Alcoholics, on my own. Daily, I woke up to understand the deceptions that I had lived under my whole life. In these meetings, people talked about their childhood experiences, sharing the rawness and struggles they faced as children of alcoholics and the devastating effects they now experienced as adults. I felt validated hearing stories that were familiar to my own experiences. These strangers were like me, at least the part of me that had grown up in an alcoholic home. At the second meeting I attended, I knew I had to say something, or I would explode. I felt so free after speaking up that I did a couple cartwheels right there in the parking lot as I was walking back to my car after the meeting. Those meetings gave me hope, and finally, things were making sense.

I took my recovery very seriously. I went to meetings three to four times a week and was committed to working with a sponsor on the twelve steps. This work led me to understand how abusive my marriage was. I had been praying and telling God that I would keep my vows and stay in the marriage because I believed that was His will, but if there were Biblical grounds for divorce, I would be out of there so fast my husband's head would spin–and the same for the neighbors. Still, I took it one day at a time, praying for God to release me. Daily, God gave me the strength to emotionally detach from my husband and all his rage and not get sucked into his mind games and manipulation. For six months, I prayed about this situation, but also stayed surrendered, quietly repeating in my heart *Not my will, but Thy will be done.*

One night, my husband came home late from a strip club and told me he had something important to tell me. He asked me to sit down, and then he got right down to it. He said, "I want a divorce." I sat there, speechless. He proceeded to tell me that he was destroying me and needed to end the marriage. I was surprised by this and thought to myself, *Wow, that is nice of you. That's the first nice thing you have ever done for me.* I acted sad like I was hearing bad news. I guess I didn't want to hurt his feelings with my obvious excitement because inside, I was doing back flips. God had answered my prayers and set me free from this night-mare. Over the next few weeks, I was comforted to discover that there were also Biblical grounds for ending the marriage. I was 21 years old when we split, released from a marriage right out of the pit of hell.

I needed a job, but I didn't have a car, so I had to find something close enough to where I was living so I could walk or ride my bike to work. One day, I walked into town and discovered that a health food store had just opened up about a mile from my house. Right when I walked through the doors, I knew that's where I wanted to be. I asked to speak to the manager, and the owner came down to talk to me. He told me that they weren't hiring but to check back in a few months. I eagerly shared with him that I really wanted to work there and told him he wouldn't be sorry if he hired me. I went back every day for a week until he was so sick of me bothering him that he offered me a job.

Working at Jimbo's was a perfect fit and a key to my healing and recovery. My coworkers, my boss, and even my customers valued me and appreciated who I was, though I had the self-esteem of a gnat. On Sundays, I would go to a local Christian church across the street from my work, where I would make sure to sit in a different section every week so that no one would recognize me or talk to me. I'd get there late and leave early. The thought of getting close to church people or getting involved in church was scary, but still, I wanted to be in church.

Two years after my divorce, at the age of 23, I started dating somebody a friend had introduced me to. We started hanging out, connected quickly, and things moved along pretty fast. After only a few months, I was pregnant.

Even though the circumstances weren't ideal, I was truly happy and felt blessed to be pregnant. I wasn't scared or concerned about how it would all work out or if my boyfriend and I would stay together forever or not. I was excited and felt ready to be a mom. I lived in my own place until I was eight months pregnant, and then I moved in with the baby's father. After everything I had been through with my firstborn David, I chose to do a home birth and found a wonderful midwife. The more I learned about birth and babies, the more confident that I became that home birth would be the best and healthiest way to go for me and my child. We planned for an underwater birth and put a beautifully hand-painted horse trough in the living room two weeks before my due date. We waited with great anticipation for the moment my labor would begin; when this precious one would enter the world. This precious one would change everything for me.

Chapter 5
My Father's Gift

El Amen, Faithful God

"Know therefore that the LORD your God is God; He is the faithful God, keeping His covenant of love to a thousand generations of those who love him and keep His commandments."

—Deuteronomy 7:9

El Channum, Gracious God

"And he passed in front of Moses, proclaiming, 'The LORD, the LORD, the compassionate and gracious God, slow to anger, abounding in love and faithfulness.'"

—Exodus 34:6

"'For I know the plans I have for you,' declares the Lord, 'plans to prosper you and not to harm you, plans to give you hope and a future.'"

—Jeremiah 29:11

Nathan Adams Upton was born at home on July 12, 1988. He was an absolutely perfect and beautiful little boy. The minute he was born, the midwife put him on my belly, and we watched in awe as he inched his way up my body, moving over my chest and towards my face. Surprised, the midwife told me that she had never seen a baby do that before. It was as if Nathan knew he was deeply loved even before he was born, and he seemed to want to get as close to me as possible right away. As I lay still on the floor blown away by this incredible moment, he nuzzled his little body into my neck. It took my breath away to finally see this perfect little being, who minutes before was inside of me, on top of me. With tears, I took hold of him and held him to my breast, where he latched on effortlessly as he gazed up into my eyes.

It was love at first sight. This baby was a gift, right out of Heaven. His father and I wanted the perfect name for this precious baby boy. I prayed, asking God what his name was to be. After two weeks of waiting, we were certain. His name was Nathan– gift from God.

Nathan taught me how to love and be loved.

Up until that point, I believed that love always came with a price tag. This love, however, was different. For the first time, I felt like me–my most authentic self–pouring all my love into this beautiful baby. There wasn't a fear that it was too much or that I was too much. This love could be raw, big, and beautiful.

Having a child was like watching a dam break open and finally flow freely to where it was safe to go. This was the beginning of a whole new reality for me. Nathan taught me how to play, to laugh, to just be. I loved every minute of being his mom.

Nathan's dad and I knew we were not going to marry, and sadly, we split up when Nate was just over one year old. We were young and wanted different things in life. During this time, the decision for us to go our separate ways was excruciatingly painful. We understood it was going to be a difficult journey ahead.

I wanted to give Nathan my very best self, and in order to do that, I knew that I needed to make a dramatic change. But I still hadn't fully surrendered to Jesus. I still wanted to do things my way–until I visited a counselor who set me straight.

My mom offered to pay for me to see a female counselor from her church, someone who could help me sort through everything that had happened over the last several years. As soon as I walked into her office, I began to tell her the whole story of my failed relationship. I listed all of the reasons that, in my mind, things were the way they were in my life.

At first, she quietly listened to me. Then suddenly, she questioned me in a stern voice.

"Are you a Christian?"

Puzzled by this, I responded, "Yes!" I then proceeded to go on with my story.

She interrupted me again, this time even more sternly.

"You are not a Christian. You are a humanist."

I was stunned, speechless, shocked, and offended.

"Where is your integrity, woman?"

Now, I was angry. I began to defend myself when she interrupted me again.

"Do you even know what integrity is?" she asked me. "Integrity means that you would die for something you believe in. Where is your integrity if you are calling yourself a Christian and still holding onto sin?"

Now I was *very* angry. I began explaining more of why I was in this situation and not really taking ownership that I was rebelling against God.

"I rebuke that rebellious spirit in Jesus' name!" the counselor interrupted me yet again.

By now, I was crying tears of frustration. I wanted to run out of the room. I thought this woman was horrible. This was not the counseling I had imagined!

"Are you ready? Are you ready to surrender to God and become a *true* follower of Jesus Christ? Are you done yet? Are you ready to put your foot on the narrow path?"

I broke down and started crying, "Yes! Yes! I am ready!" She stood next to me and laid her hands on my head and began to pray over me as I surrendered my heart and life to Jesus Christ. I sat there sobbing, thanking Jesus for His love and grace for me. I surrendered my life that day to walk with the Lord and serve Him. Choosing to trust Him with my son and my life, I set my feet on the path of obedience and daily surrender.

That day, I dedicated my whole life to Jesus. I knew that being close to Him was my only hope of being the best parent I could be. and I knew God was calling me to surrender this relationship and follow Him fully.

At this time, I was in a management position at the health food store and continued to enjoy working there. My boss even allowed me to bring Nathan with me to work. I would strap him on my body and wear him to work with me every day. He'd be with me all over the store: at the register, stocking shelves, taking inventory, and talking to shoppers and other employees. I would even bundle him up, strap him to my front, throw a beanie on his head and a pair of mittens on his tiny hands, and head into the refrigerators and freezers to stock the shelves and take inventories. My coworkers loved the chance to hold Nate on their lunch break, when he was sleeping, or when I needed to give my back a rest. Nathan and I both loved being there, and it worked out well until he started to walk and wanted to explore the world, which meant our sweet little arrangement could no longer work.

After being there for five years, I had to say goodbye to the health food store and all my coworkers, who were now friends. I had never waited on tables before, but I figured I could work half the time, make good money, and have as much time with Nathan as possible. I was blessed with a great job at a popular restaurant on the harbor and started working a few nights a week.

Nathan and I had a cute little one-bedroom apartment a few blocks from the ocean. In the mornings or early evenings, depending on my work schedule, I would put him in the running stroller, and we would head down to the beach. If it wasn't the beach, we'd check out different parks or visit with friends. He was such a sweet and mellow little guy. In this experience of being a mom, I began to understand the love God has for me as His child and what life in His love was supposed to be like. The depths of love we feel as parents are endless; there is nothing I wouldn't do for my child. Being a mom helped me to realize that God feels the same way about me.

Nathan was my wonder child, and those were *my* wonder years too. My relationship with God felt all new to me. My heart was completely turning and trusting Him more and more each day. Daily I was being shown who God is as my protector, my provider, and the One who knows and loves me unconditionally. My faith was growing and my dependence on Him was deepening because I was in the position to have to rely on God for everything we needed.

When Nathan was almost two, I was ready to find a church. I felt led to see if there was a Vineyard church in the area, so I opened the white pages in the phone book and quickly found one in La Jolla not far from where we lived in Pacific Beach. I jumped into my '61 Ford Falcon with Nathan and headed there that next Sunday. After our first visit, I knew this was the church where we were supposed to be. I also knew it was important to be around people who were choosing to follow Jesus because I needed accountability. I didn't want to stray off the path or do my own thing anymore, and I knew I was capable of that. I met a few powerful and godly women at this church, prayer warriors who were also young mothers like me. I held on closely to these women, learned from them, and stayed involved in the church community in any way I could. I wanted to grow and learn to make wise and healthy choices. Nathan and I were also cared for and embraced by the people at this church. They were always willing to help me if I had to work late and needed a babysitter, and I could completely trust them with my son.

Stepping out into the world as a single mom, we had obvious needs. I needed a bed for Nate, a table and chairs for our kitchen, pots, and pans, and everything else our little apartment needed to become a home. During that time, I encountered many people with good intentions, wanting to give me advice on what I should or shouldn't do as a single mom. Others would see my need, but stay at a distance, maybe because they didn't know what to say or do. But God was showing me something very important in those days that stuck with me. I didn't need people's advice or opinions of my situation, and I definitely didn't need their judgment of my past decisions. I needed practical help; I simply needed a bed for my son. When I began to see God providing all Nate and I needed daily, it felt miraculous.

Jesus warned us in James 2:16 not to say, "Be warmed, Be filled" as they walk on by someone with a need–or to say "I'll pray for you" in a dismissing way– without ever praying. What I learned in this season was what it felt like for someone to actually give you something that you need when you need it and to actually pray when they say they will. I was experiencing practical help and love through others, and I saw that it was my Father God who was providing for me. I truly learned the meaning of the verse, "Every good and perfect gift is from above, coming down from the Father of the heavenly lights, who does not change like shifting shadows." (James 1:17) The God I knew from my upbringing was changing. My image of "father" was changing. Unlike my earthly father, this God was loving and continually present. I experienced that *all* our needs, both big and small, were important to Him. He didn't push me away or demand perfection but drew me in, practically demonstrating His love for me and my son every day. In this beautiful experience of mothering Nathan and being fathered by God, the brokenness from my childhood was finally being confronted. Healing was happening in my heart.

I've often heard the saying, "It took a long time to get to where I am; it's going to take some time to get out." As I was growing stronger in my faith, something challenging was surfacing at the same time. I started battling panic attacks when I was at work waiting on tables. It would hit me out of nowhere. Right in the middle of my shift, my heart would start racing, and my hands would shake so badly that my customers and other patrons would notice. I even lost it a few times, tossing a tray of drinks onto everyone sitting at one of my tables. However horrible this was for me, I had to keep working. We lived off my tips and a small hourly wage, so I did my best to get through each time it happened, which became more and more frequent. I became desperate for this to stop, especially when my manager pulled me aside one night and told me that I needed to pull it together or I was going to lose my job.

One night, when we were super busy and the panic started to come over me, I asked my coworker to cover my tables for a few minutes and went into the bathroom, angry that this fear was trying to ruin my life. I looked directly into the mirror, stared right into my own eyes, and said out loud, "For God has not given us a spirit of fear, but of power and of love and of a sound mind." (2 Timothy 1:7 NKJV). I said it a few more times until my body started settling down. I regained my composure and walked out of the bathroom, determined to finish my shift without another episode. The panic attack was gone.

I would have to do this pretty much every time I worked for the next few months until eventually, the attacks stopped coming altogether. God was teaching me the power of His word and how to use it like a weapon against these anxiety attacks. I started memorizing scriptures, holding onto them every day to keep me steady, like an anchor holds a ship. He was also teaching me, out of absolute necessity, to pray constantly while I was going about the busyness of the day. That was how I began to hear and recognize His voice. I felt like a baby, completely dependent on my Father for absolutely everything: my emotional, spiritual, physical, and mental needs. There were times when things weren't easy between Nathan's dad and me, which brought up a lot of anxiety as well. Daily, I was surrendering and leaning into Jesus for my every need. Being a mom and wanting the best for Nathan kept me motivated to press on.

It was during this time that God asked me to trust Him even more and start tithing. I wanted to be fully obedient to Him in everything, so I gave Him my yes and committed to giving a tenth of the money I'd earned waiting on tables each week. It might be difficult, but I felt excited about this next step.

I'll never forget the day when God asked me to give *above* 10%. Now, that was scary; it was during the slow season, and I hadn't made that much in tips. In other words, it was the perfect time to grow even greater trust in my heavenly Father. One Sunday, the Lord spoke to me, putting it on my heart to give twenty dollars to another single mother in the church.

Twenty dollars? Really? That's gas for a week, Lord! I thought. But nonetheless, I found myself standing next to her after church as if God was saying, "Let's do this." With some reluctance, I told her what the Lord had put on my heart. She broke down crying, so touched by our loving Father God, who made it clear that He saw her need and was providing for her and her two boys too. With tears, she started telling me that she didn't have any money until the first of the month, which was a few days away. She knew she had to get her and the boys to church that morning but only had enough gas to get to church, not enough to get back home. She decided to trust God that He would make a way for them to get back. Learning this story, we stood there together with our boys next to us and celebrated the goodness of God. I was thrilled; I had heard God's voice, said yes, and immediately got to see the fruit of obedience.

That night at work, I received a $93 tip from one table and another $200 from my entire shift–almost 300 bucks in one night. It was thrilling! God was teaching me to trust and to give, even out of lack. This wasn't some *give so you get* gospel like you hear television preachers sometimes talking about. This truly was my heart wanting to trust and obey God with everything, even the little bit of money I made.

I started studying whole books in the Bible, hungry to understand the Word of God. Being raised in a cult meant that I saw stories and sentences from the Bible being twisted to manipulate and control others. But God was freeing me from the cult's influence, destroying all the lies and misconceptions I believed about Him and His Word. He wanted me to know the real Him. I felt led to start studying the names of God that are written about in the Old Testament, given after the children of Israel had witnessed a miracle or had an encounter with God. These were names like *El Shaddai*, Almighty God; *Yahweh Jireh*, the God who provides; and *Yahweh Rapha*, the God who heals. I didn't know it at the time, but a focus on the names of God would become foundational to my faith over the next years of my life.

I devoured this study and became passionate about sharing it with others. Knowing His names gave me new confidence in who I am and to who I belonged to. The Word of God was finally healing me.

Chapter 6
A New Beginning

Yahweh Nissi, The LORD my Banner

"Moses built an altar and called it The LORD is my Banner."
—Exodus 17:15

El Chaiyai, God of my life

"By day the LORD directs his love, at night his song is with me- a prayer to the God of my life."
—Psalm 42:8

I met Brew when Nate was three-and-a-half years old. It was Thanksgiving of 1994 when my church and his church joined together to feed the homeless. I was running around serving people that day when I noticed this guy standing there with his guitar, looking around like he didn't know what was going on. I assumed he was homeless, probably hungry, and wanted a place to sit and eat, so I filled up a couple of plates of food, grabbed a soda, and walked over to him. When I asked him if I could help him find somewhere to sit, he smiled and told me he wasn't homeless; he was there to serve that day. We laugh about it now because we never would have met had I not believed him to be one of our visitors.

I found out later that all my friends from church knew Brew and had a lot of respect for him as a Christian man. He loved God and was sincerely devoted to Him. But they also knew him as Brewster Briggs, the famous surfer. It seemed everyone knew Brew but me. Growing up, Brew was considered one of the best surfers in California. But at 18, he had a radical encounter with Jesus and became a born-again Christian. He began sharing his faith with his friends, but sadly they were not open to the idea, and some even thought he'd lost his mind. Before he met Jesus, Brew was at the top of his surfing career and had everything anyone his age would want. But now, Jesus was number one, and his life had radically changed. He was frustrated that his friends were not jumping on board with what he was sharing, so he devoted himself to prayer and committed to daily prayer by walking over Windansea Beach in La Jolla. After about four years of faithfully doing this, his prayers were answered in a big way. Revival broke out in La Jolla, and many came to Christ. Big-name surfers with great followings and influence were getting saved, which, in turn, led many others to accept Jesus.

Brew and I dated for a year and a half before getting married on February 13,1996. He had two beautiful sons, Sean and Eric, and I had Nathan. We got pregnant with our beautiful Emily after only a few months, which brought our family closer in such a sweet way. Three years after Emily was born, our precious Lily came along–both girls in home birth, just like Nate.

Life was full. I loved being a wife and a mom. All my children felt like unique treasures, and I learned a lot in those early years while homeschooling, cooking, playing with my kids, and watching them discover who they are and what they love to do. As the kids were growing up, we continued to be part of the Windansea Surf Club and would spend a lot of time at the beach as a family. On the weekends, we would even camp along the coast of California at different surf spots where Brew would compete in surf contests.

We had a lot of fun together as a family but being a blended family of seven definitely had its challenges. It wasn't just his, mine, and ours; we also had Nate's dad and Eric and Sean's mom to think about. On top of that, finances were pretty tough. Brew worked hard as a landscape contractor to provide for our family and to pay child support for his boys, and I did everything I could to be able to stay home and bring in money, including providing childcare and taking in foreign exchange students. But one of the beautiful blessings of that time was learning creativity out of necessity–stretching a dollar when you would never guess it could go that far, making a meal for the whole family and a couple of guests out of whatever little was in the fridge, and continuing to trust the Lord for everything we needed. This season was an important teacher for me, especially for the future.

In 1998, the house we were renting went on the market. I was devastated because we loved that house, the neighborhood, and all of our friends there, but there was no way we could afford to buy it. I had hoped and dreamed it would be our home forever, but we had to move. We found a rental a block away that we were excited about because we would be able to stay in the neighborhood, but that turned out to be a nightmare. Right after we moved in, dog urine that had saturated the carpet pads from the previous tenant began surfacing throughout the whole house. We had to pack up everything and leave after only one month. At the same time, my grandma passed away and left us a little money, so we decided to take advantage of the opportunity and take a road trip to the Northwest. I was homeschooling Nathan and Emily, so it was no problem to pack up the classroom, put our belongings in storage, and hit the road. We were excited about this opportunity, as we had never traveled farther north than Sacramento. We bought an old station wagon for the trip and piled in. The kids named it "Puff the Magic Wagon" because the headliner was falling, and it was like a big puffy cloud hanging over our heads for the entire trip. Brew's boys were living with their mom at the time and didn't have the flexibility of homeschooling, which unfortunately meant they couldn't join us.

We had a wonderful adventure traveling up through California and going as far as Victoria, Canada. It was a beautiful experience full of camping, fishing, surfing, sightseeing, schooling, and reading books together as a family. This became a deeply treasured time for all of us. Before we even left for the Northwest, I had a thought that we were to stay in Oregon and not go back to San Diego. I kept thinking about the town called Bend, which sounded crazy because we'd never been there, didn't know anybody there, and had never thought about moving away from San Diego. I prayed, asking God to show me if this thought was just my idea or His plan. After reading about Gideon in the book of Judges, I put a fleece out to God. My fleece was that I wouldn't mention what I was thinking about, but if it was God's plan for us to stay in Oregon, He would show Brew.

Long story short, we went on the road trip and never went back to San Diego. While visiting a friend in Washington, Brew randomly said, "I think we need to go back through Bend and check it out." I was shocked. Shortly after, we decided to leap into a new adventure. We found an affordable apartment close to town and signed a six-month lease. Winter was already hitting us, so Brew jumped on a plane and headed to San Diego to get our things while the kids and I stayed in Bend. He rented a 27-foot truck, loaded it with everything that was in our storage, and headed back up to Oregon. Eric decided to make the trip up with his dad and live with us there, which was an answer to prayer. We called our family and friends and told them the shocking news that we were not coming back. They were both surprised and sad because there was no discussion about this possibility before we left, which meant there were no hugs and formal goodbyes with our loved ones. That was hard, but we were ready for change. We wanted to be on this adventure, and we were looking forward to whatever was next for our family. Thankfully, Nathan's dad was supportive and even came to stay with us for a couple weeks during Christmas that year.

Bend was a wonderful place to live. The boys got passes to Mount Bachelor and would jump on the afternoon shuttle and head up to the mountain each day to snowboard after they finished their studies. Emily had just turned five years old when we got to Bend and soon fell in love with gymnastics. Lily wasn't quite two years old at the time and was as sweet and funny as could be.

Brew and I both knew that we wanted to do life and church differently in Oregon. We were wanting a simpler, slower pace. We wanted to be able to have more family time, and we both desired to serve God and His people in a more intentional way. We were aware of how blessed we were and felt sure that we weren't supposed to sit in a church and *get* more, but it was time to *give* more.

Right away, we found a ministry called Set Free Refuge which was a Christ-centered drug and alcohol recovery program for men. We loved the ministry and felt God's call for us to be a part of what they were doing there. Their church building was a beautiful old barn with a big wooden cross on it. The barn sat next to a little pond where Lily and Emily loved to catch frogs every Sunday. During the regular church services, the men in the program would share their testimonies and praise reports of all God did to save them and the miracles and restoration that were happening in their lives. It was so refreshing for Brew and me to hear raw and honest stories of addiction, temptation, daily choosing life over death, and what it is like to be newly sober and walk with Jesus. These were men who were broken and had burned every bridge now hungering for God and having the courage to face the consequences of their past. We were deeply moved by their tears of thankfulness to Jesus, who had given them another chance at life. Brew led worship on Sundays and taught Bible classes in the evening, and I led a small Bible study with the wives and girlfriends of the men that were in the program.

Life was imperfect but beautiful, messy, but fun, and rich with family and God. We thought we were all set. But we had no idea what was in store next.

Chapter 7
Memorial Day

El Gibbor, Mighty God, Hero

"The LORD your God is in your midst. The mighty One will save : He will rejoice over you with gladness, He will quiet you with His love, He will rejoice over you with singing."
$\qquad$—Zephaniah 3:17 NKJV

Elohim Machase Lanu, God our Refuge

"…God is our refuge and strength, an ever-present help in trouble."
$\qquad$—Psalm 46:1

"For he will command his angels concerning you to guard you in all your ways; they will lift you up in their hands, so that you will not strike your foot against a stone."
$\qquad$—Psalm 91:11-12

In 1999, my sweet 84-year-old Aunt Bettie was woken up early Saturday morning two days before Memorial Day. She felt that the Holy Spirit was alerting her to open her Bible to Psalm 91:11-12. She wrote out the scripture word for word on a piece of paper, including the names of each person in my immediate family: *Brew, Sheri, Eric, Nathan, Emily,* and *Lily.* For the next few days, Aunt Bettie prayed that scripture over each of us by name.

That same weekend, Brew was invited to join the Windansea Surf Club to compete in the annual Steamer Lane surf contest in Santa Cruz, California. We had just retired our old station wagon, "Puff," and purchased a van–our first big *newer* car purchase. We were excited about the idea of driving to Santa Cruz to surf with friends from San Diego, and Brew couldn't wait to compete with the surf club he'd been a part of since he was 12 years old. It was a Friday night when we packed up the van and the kids and headed out of Bend. We drove through the night and arrived in Santa Cruz early Saturday morning. The drive went smoothly, and the weekend ended up being a really special time of visiting with friends, surfing, camping, and hanging out at the beach with our wonderful children. Brew surfed well, as usual, and placed third in the forty- to forty-five-year-old category. He was happy with his results, and so were we.

Early in the evening on Sunday, it was time to head back home to Oregon. With a 10-hour drive ahead of us, we packed up our camping gear and all of our things, said our goodbyes, and headed north. We drove as far as we could that night and ended up getting a motel room in a small mountain town called Dunsmuir, just a few hours south of Oregon by Mount Shasta. We woke up the next morning to the crisp mountain air and the sunlight beaming through the tall pine trees that surrounded us. It was going to be an especially beautiful day, so we decided to go on a hike to a nearby waterfall before getting back on the road. The Shasta Mountains and the clear, raging waters were breathtaking, and I caught myself slowing down to take in the moment. It felt like God was giving us a gift in every detail of that day. I was aware of the deep connection we shared as a family the entire weekend but especially *that* day. The children were happy and noticeably enjoying each other and the beauty that surrounded them. We all felt it–a near-tangible sense of peace and contentment.

Looking back, I see that was the calm before the storm that was to change our lives forever.

Leaving the Shasta Mountains, I jumped into the driver's seat for this leg of the trip, and Brew sat in the passenger seat. Eric (15), Nathan (11), Emily (5), and Lily (2), were belted in and ready for the long trip back home. We headed up the 5 Freeway towards Oregon. After about four hours of driving, I realized that I was on the wrong highway, which put us way behind schedule. Once we got back on track, Brew and I were relieved to see the signs for Highway 97, Klamath Falls, Oregon–only about two hours from home.

"It won't be long now!" we shouted to the kids. We pulled into a gas station to fuel up and get a quick snack. The kids had been in the van for a long time at that point and begged us to let them out of their car seats and seat belts so they could lie down, and we decided to go ahead and let them. Eric was the only one who stayed in his seatbelt. For this final stretch, Brew took over the driving, and I jumped into the passenger seat.

It was a warm, clear summer night. With our seat belts off, the windows rolled down, shorts and tank tops on, and my bare feet up on the dashboard, we sang as loud as we could to a Rolling Stones song that was playing on the radio. I remember looking out, taking in the incredible beauty that surrounded us. Heading north on the highway, Klamath Lake was to the left. I noticed how the evening sun was shining down on the calm water, making it sparkle. On our right were towering mountains dotted with lava rocks. Though we had gotten a little lost, the drive was beautiful, and life felt good.

At around 5:40 PM, we'd traveled about five miles since our last stop on Highway 97. We were cruising along at approximately 55 mph when suddenly a car pulled into our lane and was heading right towards us. I screamed, totally aware that we had nowhere to go on this narrow two-lane highway. We couldn't escape the inevitable. Brew swerved hard to the right, trying to miss the oncoming vehicle but was unable to. We hit the left front side of the car heading towards us, flew straight up in the air, came down, and hit the side rail on the right side of the road. Then our entire vehicle flipped three more times, throwing Brew, me,

Nathan, Emily, and Lily out of the car and directly onto the highway. I felt my body SLAM, SLAM, and SLAM again. I remember feeling the first impact and then the sensation of my body being tossed and bashed onto the pavement again and again.

It felt as if it was all happening in slow motion. I remember the moments in between impact when I was still airborne, and then I'd slam against something again. I remember thinking, "This is a big crash. When is this going to stop?" It felt like it kept going on and on. Oddly, I felt as if I was in a bubble, protected while being tossed around like a rag doll. Finally, there was a stillness and quiet so loud that I will never forget it. I sat up from where I had landed on the highway and looked down at my legs in front of me, bruised and bloodied. Then, I looked out towards the lake to see the sun still hovering in the sky above. On the lake side of the highway, the van had landed on its popped tires. I didn't know it at the time, but Brew was stuck underneath, his head half an inch from being crushed under the wheel well. I had landed fifty feet across from the van, opposite the lake at the base of the mountain. Miraculously, three of my beautiful children landed alongside me like ducks in a row. My baby, Lily, landed on my right side within arm's reach. Nathan was next to me on my left, and Emily landed about 25 feet away from the three of us. Eric had his seatbelt on and was still inside the van. As I sat there looking out on the water, I sensed a holy hush in the air; all was still, quiet, and surreal. I looked down at my bloody legs again but felt confidence in me and around me.

"No weapon formed against me will prosper!" I declared loudly and boldly. They were the very first words to come out of my mouth after the crash.

And then with no effort or panic whatsoever, I began praying and speaking life and healing over my family, naming them one by one. I was aware that this reaction to what just happened and the power surging through my broken body were absolute miracles. The third miracle was that I was alive and I somehow knew that my family was alive too. I reached over and gently scooped my two-year-old baby Lily onto my lap. She was quiet, almost asleep. I spoke softly to her, pulling her close to my chest. I heard Nathan moaning to the left of me. I reached out and laid my hand on him. He was face down, lying on his stomach. I told him with a soft voice and with complete confidence that he was okay and that we were going to be okay. I couldn't see Emily, so I yelled her name. She didn't answer. I yelled out with a strength and authority not of my own, "Emily, wake up in the name of Jesus!" I heard her cry in the distance and knew she was okay too.

All my children should have been dead, but I had no doubt they were not only alive but well. I didn't know it at the time, but a nurse was traveling two cars back from us and ran from her car to care for Emily and make sure she didn't move in case her neck was broken. By now, cars had stopped, and people were getting out to surround our family. Complete strangers knelt beside me and my children, praying and assuring me that God was with us. These were prayer warriors, people of compassion that had witnessed my family flying out of our van onto the highway.

I believe they were divinely set up to be with us that day. I didn't have any fear or doubt. As a matter of fact, I felt very much alive in those moments. I've described it this way: it was as if *what could not be shaken, was not shaken.* What was there was fierce, focused, and powerful. It was Jesus, alive inside of me, the One who cannot be shaken. Out there on Highway 97, I knew we were surrounded by the host of angels described in Psalm 91 and prayed for by my Aunt Bettie. I continued to pray out loud and with confidence while my eyes searched for Brew and Eric. A man came up to me and told me that Brew was on the other side of the highway. We didn't know if he was dead or alive, but we knew that help was on the way. Then, I spotted my oldest son getting out of the van. In complete shock, Eric started walking around barefoot on the highway full of glass and broken car parts. He looked confused and scared, searching for his family members spread out over the asphalt.

"Eric, we are over here! We are okay," I yelled to him. Worried about his feet, I asked him to get his shoes on.

"Where's dad?" he asked.

I didn't know. Finally, Eric found Brew under the van laying still in a pool of blood. He didn't know if he was dead or alive at that point, and in a panic, he began to try to lift the van off of his dad. The man in the car that was directly behind us came running to help him, and soon another man jumped in to help as well. The two men were able to lift the van off of Brew as Eric grabbed hold of his dad's ankles and pulled him out from under the now-totaled vehicle. Brew was unconscious, bloodied, and broken from head to toe. But I knew he would be okay. It was then that I began to hear the sounds of sirens in the distance getting louder as they approached us.

Thankfully we were only five miles from the nearest hospital, and Brew was taken first, right to the ICU. They took my children two by two in separate ambulances and I followed, alone. The paramedics strapped me down to a gurney so I couldn't move, and upon arriving at the hospital, they put me in a room by myself. My children were together in the room adjacent. X-rays and exams for the children first, as I lay covered in glass and gravel next door, waiting to hear if the kids had any broken bones or serious injuries. I lay there, listening to their cries, frustrated that I couldn't get to them. I even called their names through the wall, hoping they could hear me and my voice would bring them some comfort.

After being thoroughly checked, the children were placed in whirl-pool baths to help clean out any of the gravel and glass that entered through their cuts and scrapes. Beyond that, the extent of their injuries was minimal. Eric had five stitches in one of his fingers. Emily had a slight break in the growth plate of her arm, plus some gravel and glass that needed removing in two small areas. Nathan had road rash from head to toe on the left side of his body, but only superficially; not a single scar would remain. My two-year-old, Lily, had nothing that the doctors could see: no broken bones, cuts, bruises, or scrapes. After flying over fifty feet and landing on the highway, their injuries were so minor that they would be released that evening from the hospital.

In the meanwhile, I begged the doctor to unstrap me from the gurney and allow me to see my children. He didn't want to until I had been examined, not wanting to risk further injury in case my neck was broken. Finally, I convinced him that I would stay absolutely still if he removed the restraints. When he agreed, I broke my promise and immediately began twisting my neck around, indicating that it was completely fine–another miracle.

After a few hours, the nurses wheeled me in to see my precious children. I was so grateful for how tender and loving the nurses and other staff had been with them, caring for their wounds and hearts so gently. Still, it was clear they needed their mama. When they saw me, we all broke into tears of joy, more than sorrow. We were together and alive. I spoke to each one, assuring them.

"We're all going to be okay–and daddy is going to be okay too!" I continued, "God is with us. He's been with us this whole time."

My children simply looked at me and nodded. They knew, and I knew. God was with us, just as He promised He would be. He was our refuge and our fortress, our God in whom we trusted. Psalm 91:2.

My family and I had just lived through the greatest miracle I had ever seen or heard about, and we were at the center of it.

As we slowly recovered, we began to make decisions about what to do next. I called my mother and told her about what happened. Then I asked that she call a friend of ours in Bend, Paul Frazier. I knew he would know what to do, and sure enough, he did.

Without any hesitation at all, Paul left his family and headed to Klamath Falls to take care of things for us. He managed our now-totaled vehicle and thoroughly searched the entire area where the accident had happened, gathering our possessions one by one. He even found my glasses in a nearby bush and the new skateboards we had bought our boys that weekend.

Meanwhile, we rested and recovered in the hospital. I was black and blue from head to toe and had glass and gravel throughout my entire body. I had a few broken ribs, an injured sternum, a broken left foot, a broken right toe, and ripped tendons in my left foot. At around 11 PM the night of the crash, I had to go into surgery to remove all the glass and gravel from my body. I told the staff I did not want to go under anesthesia because I wanted to be awake and alert for my kids when my surgery was finished. They gave me just enough to prevent severe pain and keep me unconscious during the duration of the surgery. Turns out, it wasn't quite enough; I remember frequently waking up to the sounds of "Good Vibrations" and other classic Beach Boy songs playing in the background. Meanwhile, they pulled out over three hundred pieces of glass in my left leg alone. Needless to say, there was plenty more for the surgeons to find everywhere else.

Throughout the entire situation, the nurses and staff at Klamath Falls Hospital were extraordinarily kind and attentive. There was one nurse, however, who really stood out. Julie Brown was the head nurse on the floor to which we were ultimately transferred and was like an absolute "mama bear" to my family and me. Julie had been a missionary overseas for years before working at the hospital and had eight children of her own. That being said, Julie knew just what to do to take charge.

Throughout the days we spent at the hospital, I could feel Julie's strength and deep understanding of everything we were facing, which of course, comforted me enormously. Even though our children were not admitted into the hospital like Brew and me–because they suffered fewer injuries– she took a huge risk and directed her staff to take care of my children as though they were admitted and to treat them as if they were their own. She even put beds together, creating a bed big enough for Lily, Emily, and me to share and put the boys in the next room. Strict orders were given from Nurse Brown: my children were to be given whatever they needed or asked for. She even rallied other nurses and members in her church to pray for us and to gather clothes so we would have something to wear when we were discharged. It was–and is–clear to me: God had planned for her to be with us in such a critical and traumatic time.

On the third day after the crash, Brew was still in a coma, and I suddenly became very weak. No matter how hard I tried, I could not keep my eyes open. Not only that, but I felt dizzy and vomited continuously. Lily, my baby, was struggling as well. She couldn't stay awake and definitely wasn't acting like herself. The kids were having nightmares, and the girls and I did not have an appetite or even a desire to drink water.

A group of doctors came into my room, asking me questions about Brew and his personality. His brain injury was serious, and they wanted to know more about him to help make a correct assessment. I tried to answer their questions but couldn't speak myself. They asked me to stand up and see if I could walk with my crutches, but every time I'd try, I would feel nauseous. I remember the top of my head feeling strange and cold, and when I reached up to feel my scalp, my fingers sank into a huge gash. I pulled my hand away to see fresh blood and the nurse who was next to me saw it and began moving quickly and nervously. I guess they had missed that one with so many other injuries they had to deal with. I was rushed to another part of the hospital for a more thorough examination, and I ended up with 15 staples in my head. Then, they decided to do a CT scan on Lily, where they found she had a fractured skull, though it was slight and there was very little bleeding. I was further encouraged when the doctors told me that the injury occurred in the best possible place it could have and that she would be okay.

Meanwhile, Paul Frazier went to the hospital to see us that day and was alarmed by how out of it I was. Julie, our "mama bear" nurse, told us about the doctors' concerns about Brew's brain injury and their doubts about his recovery. So, Paul began to alert different churches in Klamath Falls about our condition, urging them to pray for our total recovery. In fact, the whole town knew about our crash from the news channels, and it had become quite a story that we had survived such a brutal crash. Paul decided to take it a step further and drive around Klamath Falls, walking directly into church meetings and telling them we needed immediate prayer. People responded and began to pray and intercede for us.

That entire day, I felt like I was going to die. But at 10 PM, I remember waking up from my sleep. Immediately, I knew it was gone. Whatever it was, the heaviness, sickness, and pain were totally gone. I started thanking God, knowing He had touched me. He had healed me.

Yet another huge miracle.

On the fourth day after the crash, Brew came out of the coma. Julie came in to tell me that they would be putting him in the room next to mine and asked if she could take me to see him. It would be the first time we would see each other since before the crash. They warned me that he would not look like himself. Julie pushed me in the wheelchair into his room with my two girls on my lap and the boys walking next to me. A few doctors and nurses were crowded in the room, waiting for the moment we would all see each other again.

Brew was seriously beaten up from head to toe. It was difficult even to recognize him with his swollen, broken face and bloodshot eyes. Still, he smiled when he saw me.

"Did you feel Him?" he asked.

Though he could not remember a thing about the accident–even after we told him again and again–He knew God was there. He had felt His power.

The kids and I were released to go home to Bend the next day, but Brew was to stay in the hospital another week or more to have his jaws wired shut. Every bone in his face was broken along with many other broken bones throughout his entire body.

Of course, it was difficult to say goodbye to Brew and to the doctors and nurses who had taken such good care of us. They told us they had seen many victims of car accidents on winding mountain roads on Highway 97. But this time, the family was alive. All of them. We were the miracle family, the fulfillment of Aunt Bettie's prayers.

"If you say, 'The Lord is my refuge,' and you make the Most High your dwelling, no harm will overtake you, no disaster will come near your tent. For he will command his angels concerning you to guard you in all your ways. They will lift you up in their hands, so that you will not strike your foot against a stone."

—Psalm 91:9-12

Chapter 8
The Adjuster

Yah, God who rides upon the clouds

Sing to God, sing praise to His name: Extol Him who rides on the clouds, By His name YAH, And rejoice before Him.
—Psalm 68:4 NKJV

El Roi, God who sees me

"She gave this name to the LORD who spoke to her; 'You are the God who sees me,' For she said, 'I have now seen the One who sees me.' That is why the well was called Beer Lahai Roi: it is still there, between Kadesh and Bered."
—Genesis 16:13-14

A couple days after returning home, we became very concerned for Lily. She was lethargic and weak, not eating very much, and barely talking. My brother, sister-in-law, and mom had come to Bend to take care of us and took Lily to the pediatrician. She was found to be severely dehydrated and was admitted to the hospital once again.

Needless to say, Lily didn't need this. They poked and prodded at her, struggling to get an IV and a catheter into her little body, which traumatized her all over again after the accident. She needed me, and although I could barely move because of the two casts on my legs–on top of all the other injuries–I came to the hospital to stay with her.

You can't imagine the look on the nurses' faces when they saw me on crutches, black and blue from head to toe, with two casts and bloodshot eyes. I looked like I needed to be admitted myself. The hospital would not allow my mom to stay with us, so I was on my own to care for Lily and myself. Once Lily finally fell asleep around 9 PM, I realized that I had to go to the bathroom. There was one problem with that; I could not get up by myself. I rang the nurse. I waited and then rang again. I was starting to feel a little panicked, so I continued to ring the nurse incessantly, thinking that eventually someone would come in and help. About 15 minutes went by before a nurse poked her head in and made her intentions clear, saying, "Lily is my patient, and you are not. I cannot take care of you tonight. Maybe you shouldn't be here."

Somehow, I mustered up all my strength and determination and made it to the bathroom and back. Exhausted and weary, feeling vulnerable, and worrying about my other children at home without me, I started to experience a panic attack. Though I hadn't had this kind of experience since my waitressing days, I began to feel anxiety rise up in my chest. The bandages under my casts that were covering my stitches and wounds started to irritate me to the point where I felt I had to get the casts and bandages off immediately. Thank God it was the kind of cast you could take off and on, or I would have looked for a saw. I began furiously unwrapping my bandages, obsessed and panicking. I continued ringing the bell, calling and begging the nurse to come in because I needed new bandages, but there was no response. Finally, a different nurse came in, saw the terror in my eyes, brought me a fresh wrap for my legs, and suggested that I take some deep breaths. She informed me that was all she could do, letting me know I was not her patient. With my voice desperate and trembling, as if she had just rescued me off the side of a cliff, I told her, "Thank you. Thank you for helping me. Thank you for these bandages. I won't say anything to anyone. God bless you!"

Like a crazed woman, I proceeded to unwrap and rewrap my legs all through the night. Wrap, and then unwrap, over and over again. I knew I couldn't get to the bathroom again, so I resisted any need to go and fought through the long night of panic attacks, staying awake and alert until daybreak.

One of the biggest things that saved me and kept me from losing my mind completely was a Christian channel on TV, which had worship music playing all through the night. When I saw the first signs of daybreak out of my window, I cried, relieved that the terror was over. I had made it through one of the darkest and scariest nights of my life, at least up to that point. Due to the trauma of the crash, I would have to battle claustrophobia and panic attacks for many years to come.

The next morning, the doctor came to check on Lily. He was so kind and concerned for both of us, which meant a lot to me after what I'd been through the night before. He released Lily to go home, and without me having to ask, he offered to take a look at the stitches that needed to come out of my face and feet. He even volunteered to remove them, which saved me a trip back to the hospital. I was grateful for his kindness.

Meanwhile, the WindanSea surf club of La Jolla joined together and put on a surf contest to raise money for our family to be able to survive financially for a while. Their love and generosity blew our minds. My close friends in San Diego had garage sales to raise funds too. Local churches and schools in Bend put together meal plans that would cover us for a few months. Caring people whom we'd never met before were dropping off food and wanting to meet *the family who survived the horrible crash*. We were on news stations and in the newspapers; we were the talk of the town. We even ended up meeting people who had been on Hwy 97 that Memorial Day and had witnessed my family flying through the air, not knowing if what they were seeing were bodies, blankets, or something else. Others were stuck in traffic for hours because of the crash, sitting on the two-lane highway and waiting to get home after the holiday weekend.

Brew's jaw was wired shut about a week after we left Klamath Falls. Then, he was transported by ambulance to the local hospital in Bend and placed in rehab for another month. They had Brew doing four different types of rehab therapy while he was in the hospital. What a relief that he was close to home and not in Klamath Falls any longer, so we could see him every day. He had numerous broken bones and severe road rash all over his body, but worst of all was the injury to the short-term memory part of his brain. He could not remember anything that had happened or anything I would say three seconds after I said it. Thank God that Brew is resilient. He always has a strong faith in God and a positive attitude. Even with broken bones in both feet, he proved to the nurses that he could go to the bathroom by himself. They tested him by seeing if he could stand on one foot and not fall down for ten seconds, and if he could, they would allow him to go. I said to one of the nurses, "That's the test? Can you at least blindfold him or put him on a balance beam instead? He's a big wave surfer and can balance on anything, even with broken bones."

Sure enough, he passed the test with no problem.

A couple weeks after the crash, we were notified that the insurance adjuster would be coming over to our house to give us the pay-off check for the van. I heard a knock at the door and hobbled over on my crutches to welcome him in. He stood there looking at me, holding back tears.

I thought, *This is kind of strange.*

Finally, he spoke. "I'm here to tell you the most incredible story you'll ever hear."

I thought to myself, *Is this the insurance guy or someone else?*

Then, he began to share his story.

"I was the driver in the car directly behind you when you crashed," he started.

My jaw dropped.

"I witnessed the whole thing. It took me everything I had to keep from crashing into your car, trying to stop. I saw everything. I was the one who helped lift the van off your husband. My wife was the one who called 911."

I couldn't believe it. Our insurance adjuster was right behind us when we crashed. Now, he was standing right in front of me, ready to tell me about the moments that would change our lives forever. Unbelievable. I was able to sit and listen to the story of God's love and intervention for our family in a whole new light. I learned things I would have never known because I was in the crash, flying through the air, unaware of all that was going on. This made the story all the more powerful and miraculous. We sat together and talked for a couple of hours, and I learned how radical it was for those who were there that day and witnessed the crash. He told me how we hit the other car, shot straight up like a rocket into the air about three car lengths, slammed against the railing on the right side of the road, and flipped three times as we were all thrown out onto the highway. I heard the violent, yet heavenly details of the entire experience. The fact that this guy was in my house, telling me all of this, represented the final mind-blowing miracle to me: God saw the entire thing unfold, His hand was on us, and He remained with us even in the details of the aftermath.

Chapter 9
Yes, Lord

El Emet, God of Truth

"Into Your hand I entrust my spirit; You have redeemed me, Lord, God of truth."

—Psalm 31:5 NASB

Yehovah - Yahweh Ori, God my Light

"The LORD is my light and my salvation- whom shall I fear? The LORD is the stronghold of my life- of whom shall I be afraid?"

—Psalm 27:1

We continued to heal and recover, but I was having terrible headaches that would last all day long, every day. I was frustrated because I could not afford to be in pain; my family needed me. I remember sitting at the kitchen table, looking at the tall stack of medical bills in front of me, and crying out to God. "Please God, I need to be able to function. Jesus, will you take this headache from me?" Yet another miracle: the headache stopped.

That was the last day I had one of those horrible headaches. What a huge relief to have that pain lifted off of me and to be able to think clearly.

Because of God's amazing grace, Brew healed from his many broken bones and road rash but still struggled with his memory. Or let's say, *I* struggled with his memory. The fact is, because of Brew's head injury, he couldn't remember anything that had just happened. In our day-to-day living, I couldn't rely on my husband to remember anything that was said to him, what we were involved in that day, or what our kids were up to. To make it even more challenging, Brew was unaware that he had memory issues because of the head trauma. Life is good and pretty simple when a lot of you is checked out, even if your body is banged up. As soon as he could, Brew wasted no time in getting his little boat out on the river to go fishing with our dog Belle. But I, on the other hand, had a different reality.

I felt and remembered everything that happened the day of the crash and every day that followed, which was both wonderful and challenging. I am truly blessed and grateful to have the memory of all God did for each of us that day. Because I remember, I get to share how wonderful and powerful He is. The difficult part was having to be the *one* to remember *everything* our family needed or was involved in while dealing with my own injuries and trauma–the broken bones, the reliving of the crash every time I was in a car, the PTSD, and the quirks that go along with it, the children's night terrors, doctor appointments, etc.

Not having my husband remember for me and with me was hard. But even though our new reality involved lots of challenges, we were running on "Holy Fumes." We had just experienced the biggest miracle of our lives. We might as well have walked through the "Parting of the Red Sea." Every day, we were in awe and amazement of the Almighty God who saved us. The miracles didn't stop there either. Daily, we were seeing God moving on our behalf; financial provision, physical healing, and answered prayers were non-stop. We had been made aware on Highway 97 that what is unseen in the natural is greater than what is seen. Our armor was dinged up, but our faith had been catapulted to a whole new level. There was no doubt that our lives had been spared for a reason. The only thing we could say was, "Whatever you want us to do Lord, we will do it."

At that point, we had been serving at Set Free ministries for about a year. Having only a men's home at the time, the ministry now saw a huge need for a recovery home for women. They asked us to pray about opening and running the women's home, which meant living with the women, all of us together, 24/7. The women that we would bring in would be committing to a six-month program where they would stay clean and sober. In some cases, our residents would be doing this program instead of doing prison time.

It had only been about six months since the crash, but we prayed and agreed to step into it. Looking back now, I think we could have used a little more time, but as I said, we were running on *holy fumes*.

As the date got closer for our family to move into the home, I began to get fearful about this decision. A couple weeks before the big move, I heard about a missionary visiting from Africa who would be preaching at a local church that Sunday. This guy felt called by God to come to America to evangelize and encourage Americans in their faith. That sounded interesting to me, so I made plans to go and maybe sit in the back. Right when I stepped foot into the church, however, I heard the preacher yell out to the crowd, "Who is tired of going around and around the mountain? Who is ready to step into where God is leading you? Who wants to let go of fear and enter their promised land?"

I immediately went forward, laid face down on the ground at the front of the church, and started to cry. I had a lot of thoughts swirling around, and I needed to get honest with God. I told the Lord that I was afraid. Part of me wanted to commit to the woman's home, but the other part was scared and wanted to run. Very gently, He asked me why I was afraid. I felt His deep compassion and His kind nudging. I needed to get real and share my fears and the sadness that was coming up for me. As I started to speak quietly to God, the core issue became clear.

I don't trust you.

It didn't make sense to say that after He had saved all of our lives in a car crash just a few months before. He had shown Himself trustworthy.

He made His angelic hosts known to us and provided for us abundantly. But there still was a deep fear in me.

I don't know if I can trust you, I said quietly in my heart. *A lot of bad things have happened on your watch. I don't know if my children will be safe.*

As I lay there talking to God, the terror of growing up in a home filled with addiction and abuse was surfacing. *A lot of bad stuff happened when I was a child. Why didn't you prevent it? You are God. You could have stopped it.*

He was so gentle with me as I broke down in tears right there on the floor of the church. He tenderly answered in a still, small voice in my heart, *I did not do that to you. I hate what happened to you. That was not Me or My will. Your parents did not listen to Me. My ways bring peace and not evil.*

Something happened in my heart that day. I experienced a paradigm shift. I was able to see that God never hurt me. My father's rebellion, sin, and addiction did. My mother's fear and codependency muted the wisdom of God, and because of that, life got ugly and difficult. It was clear to me at that moment that bad things happen when we don't listen to our Creator and go off in our own will and direction. Alcoholics Anonymous calls that *self will run riot.* It tries to destroy everything in its path. This truth and understanding became a profound reality for me.

As I lay there, face down on the ground, God asked me to trust Him. I said *yes.*

My husband and I and our four kids moved into a large home that was now officially open to women who wanted to get sober and change their lives. We had anywhere from two to seven women at a time. Some of the women knew Jesus and some did not. But all of them would meet Him on their road to recovery.

Every day at 6 AM, we enjoyed morning devotions in Proverbs. We ate meals together, worshiped, did Bible study, and completed chores. The women took classes. On top of that, I had one-on-one time with each of the women. It was beautiful. My children loved it, and we had a front-row seat to see many miracles and witnessed many lives change.

But it was definitely challenging at times. Disappointments and heartache would come, especially when one of the ladies would choose to go back out to the abusive, painful way that led them to our home in the first place.

One girl who was brought into our program was a meth addict with multiple felony charges. She was given the opportunity to come into our home instead of doing prison time in another state, and this was her last chance to succeed. I was pretty nervous about this one, but God's direction to me was, *You just love these women. I will do the disciplining.*

This young gal, a successful con artist, sized me up as a sweet, naive, Christian woman whom she could easily con. She came into our home and was very charming and seemingly dedicated to working on her recovery. She was up early for Proverbs every morning and always faithful to do her chores, her homework, and whatever else was asked of her. After hitting her 30-day mark, we thought all was going well with her recovery and with her relationship with God until one Thursday night.

At about 8:00 PM, a police car pulled up to the front of the house. I opened the door and without saying a word, two officers walked right in, straight through the house to the women's room, handcuffed our new resident, walked her outside, and put her in the back of a police car.

We watched from the window, completely shocked.

The parole officer came back into the house and explained to us that there had been a raid that evening at what we thought was her ex-boyfriend's house. This was the guy the court had placed a criminal restraining order on, mandating that the two of them could not be within 100 feet of each other. He was also a felon and a meth addict, and they had been partners in crime for a couple years before she had come into the women's home. During the raid, the parole officer had gone into this man's apartment. When she tried to move through the narrow pathways piled high with stuff, she reached her hand up to the top of a stack of boxes to steady herself and placed her hand on some papers. She grabbed ahold of them and discovered they were all letters this girl had written and dated after each night the couple had been together after we had all gone to sleep. The letters described what they did together and where they would meet after she would sneak out. All the detailed evidence was in plain view and written by her own hand. Busted.

The plan now was that she was going to be put on a bus the next morning and sent out of state as a felon, facing five years in prison. We were sad–and confused–that all this was going on right under our noses, but I quickly remembered what God had told me. *Just love her.* He would do the busting. Long story short, she had to stay in jail for a couple weeks before her court date. It was there in her cell that she realized that it was God who had exposed her lies. She thought she had all her bases covered. But because of the way the truth was exposed, there was no doubt in her mind that there is a God. She got down on her knees in her cell and repented and surrendered, knowing fully she couldn't con God. She couldn't pull the wool over His eyes, the way she had done to us. She turned her heart over to Jesus that day, and this time it was for real.

On her court date, she stood before the judge and admitted her guilt. But she also told him how she met Jesus in her jail cell, and that this time, she wanted to change and live her life differently. Believe it or not, the judge believed her and released her back to us, giving her one last chance. With her record, we couldn't believe it; no one could. But God had a different plan–a plan of mercy, which only drew her closer to Him.

The Bible says that it's His kindness that leads us to repentance (Romans 2:4). One look at this young woman, and we all knew she was different. When she returned to our home, she was in love with Jesus. Her eyes were full of love, her face had softened, and her countenance completely changed. I was brought to tears many times, standing in church, watching her worship Jesus with so much adoration and gratitude for saving her. Her boyfriend ended up doing jail time after the raid, and he too met Jesus. They were married a couple years later and have continued in their faith. The whole family was transformed from bondage and addiction to freedom and life.

We lived in the women's home for a year and a half before we decided it was time to move into our own place. God provided another leader to step in to live with the women, and we remained involved with the ministry. Our new house was within walking distance of the women's home, Brew continued to lead worship and lead Bible studies, and I spent time with the women one on one.

We received a small settlement from the crash, leaving us with $20,000 after all the medical bills had been paid. It was just enough for a down payment for our first home purchase of $93,000. It was a cute little house with lots of potential and close to town. It even had a two-story playhouse for the girls. We always wanted to be able to buy a home and knew this opportunity was another miracle.

Because of everything we had been through and all the ways I witnessed the hand of God in our lives–seeing daily the ways He provided, sustained, and healed–my faith grew. I was open, ready, and willing. I felt a calling; something big and brewing that God was preparing me for. I was excited about something I didn't yet understand or see but felt inside of me. Our yes to God brought anticipation for Him to use us in whatever way He wanted.

God began to give me pictures and visions of a big place–like a warehouse–that was filled with furniture and other things that people who are starting out with nothing might need. I began to write, journal, and draw pictures of what I was envisioning. Those were sweet and intimate times, dreaming with God about what this could be. I would wake up in the middle of the night and write down what I was seeing and hearing. It was exciting! I didn't share this with anyone, not even Brew. I just kept it between me and God, knowing that something was coming. God was on the move, yet again.

Chapter 10
Trusting God in the Heartbreak

El Elyon, Most High God

"The LORD Almighty has sworn, 'Surely, as I have planned, so it will be, and as I have purposed, so it will happen.'"
—Isaiah 14:24

Yehovah Uzzi, God my Strength

"The LORD is my strength and my shield; my heart trusts in Him, and He helps me . . ."
—Psalm 28:7

Life was good. My children were happy, and we were all settling into Bend as our new home. Eric and Nathan were snowboarding every winter, and Emily was homeschooling, loving gymnastics, and enjoying her new friends from the gym. Lily, only 4, started homeschooling with her brothers and sister. We would get up early, do our devotions, and start school early so the boys could catch the 11 AM shuttle up to Mount Bachelor. When Emily would go to the gym each afternoon, Lily and I had time together alone. In the evenings, the kids would finish up what schoolwork they didn't get done earlier in the day. It worked out perfectly. Brew always had plenty of work in Bend, and after work and on the weekends, he was busy working on our new house. Nathan spent time with his dad in San Diego during the summer and winter breaks, but he lived with us during the regular school year.

In the winter of 2001, Nathan went to see his dad down in San Diego for a two-week winter break. While he was there, his dad called to inform me that Nathan was not coming home but was going to stay with him in San Diego. He let me know, very clearly, that it was his turn to have Nate full-time.

On hearing this, my stomach turned, and my nervous system immediately went into overdrive. I knew Nathan would not want to be abruptly moved to a new school and home without having a chance to say goodbye to his friends. He would not want to be far away from us. He loved being a big brother to his sisters, and he loved his life in Bend. He loved his dad, of course, but home had always been with us. I thought, *Not now. Not yet. He's 13 and it's right in the middle of the school year.*

But there was no plan B as far as his dad was concerned. This decision was simply the way it was going to be, according to him.

So I did the only thing I knew to do: I got down on my knees and cried out to God. I didn't know what to pray, what to think, or what to do. I just knew I needed God's help. The next day, I woke up feeling like I had the flu because of the stress. I rolled out of bed and got down on my knees again, surrendering to God saying, *If this is your will, I will do it. You know more than I do about what is best for Nathan, and I want only the very best for my son. But if it is not Your will, I'm going to fight with everything in me.*

I didn't know how I would receive a clear answer. I knew I wouldn't see something specific in the Scriptures, like "Nathan is to stay in San Diego." But I was desperate to hear from God and in a hurry too.

Knowing our history, I was aware that his dad and I were not going to be able to work out a compromise.

A few days later, on a Sunday, I woke up with a clear direction. I heard the Holy Spirit tell me to visit a church that I had never gone to before. How great is the grace and love of God that made it even possible for me to hear this! I didn't know anything about this church or anybody who went there, but I had seen a flyer for a harvest festival that a little church in Tamalo, Oregon had put on a couple months before. I told Brew, who was supposed to be leading worship that morning at Set Free. He looked at me like, *What are you thinking? We are supposed to be at Set Free in 30 minutes.*

Thankfully, he prayed and heard the Holy Spirit say to go with me. We quickly canceled with Set Free, got the kids dressed, and all jumped in the car. Half an hour later, we pulled up to a tiny yellow chapel that felt like it was in the middle of nowhere. Feeling like we were on a scavenger hunt, we walked in and sat down in the back row closest to the door. By that time, we were about 15 minutes late to service, and there were only about 20 people.

When the morning worship time was just finishing up, the pastor began to walk back and forth at the front of the church, while the people sat quietly waiting for him to say something. He had a serious look as he paced. After a few minutes, he said, "There is someone here who is in pain and turmoil over her son." I reached over and grabbed Brew's hand in a tight grip and sat straight up in my seat as tears began streaming down my face.

"You keep crying out to God saying, 'Thy will be done. Thy will be done,' over and over again," he continued. "Your son is not with you right now, but the Lord has heard your prayers. The Lord is saying to you, 'My will is being done. I have placed him where he is to be right now, with specific mentors and for a specific season and purpose. My will is being done. You have given him to Me, you have taught him of Me, and he will walk with Me.'"

The pastor's last words to me were, "God wants you to know, you will always be his mama."

Every prayer and every cry to God, alone in my bedroom or driving in my car, were answered at that moment. I could not believe how specific his words were to me in such a desperate time. As a result, indescribable peace and calm came over me immediately. I knew without a doubt what God was asking me to do. I stopped fighting and surrendered.

It was not easy. My heart broke that day as I knew I had to let go of Nathan to live in another state. I felt like I sacrificed my son and surrendered my will, and only by faith was I able to do it. If it wasn't for such a radical encounter, a *word of knowledge* revealing my own words and prayers through a stranger, I would never be able to do this. But that moment, in that little church, God revealed to me that Nathan was in San Diego for a purpose and a plan bigger than my own. What could I do but believe and say, *Not my will, but Thy will be done?*

I called Nate's dad the next day and let him know I was not going to fight this.

Nathan was hurt in the beginning and didn't understand why he would have to suddenly leave Bend, his family, and his friends. I had to remain strong and affirming, trusting this was going to bless Nathan in the long run. I simply chose to hold on to all the Holy Spirit said through a stranger in that little yellow chapel, so undeniable.

God had answered my cry, spoke to me clearly, and once again, He gave me peace in the storm.

Chapter 11
Tested

Yahweh Rapha, The LORD who Heals

"If you listen carefully to the LORD your God and do what is right in his eyes, if you pay attention to his commands and keep all his decrees, I will not bring on you any of the diseases I brought on the Egyptians, for I am the LORD, who heals you."
—Exodus 15:26

Elohim Azar, God our Helper

"Surely God is my help; the Lord is the one who sustains me."
—Psalm 54:4

Finally, everything began to catch up with me. PTSD that I didn't know I had from the car crash, combined with saying goodbye to Nate caused my body to begin to show signs of stress, and I started to get sick. I was also battling insomnia, which didn't help.

During this challenging time, I committed to writing every scripture on healing from both the Old and New Testaments. I needed to be healed, and I wanted to clearly understand what God's Word says about healing, so I wrote each scripture out word for word in my journals while my body felt like it was literally falling apart. But every time I would get a new sickness or be diagnosed with something, God would heal me. Often, He would do it in different ways.

The first illness that hit me after Nathan moved to San Diego was diverticulitis. I had been in an incredible amount of pain with an on-and-off fever for a couple of weeks, so I decided to go to the ER. Because I was only 37 years old at the time, the doctors didn't suspect diverticulitis, but after a CT scan, they found it. The antibiotics they prescribed didn't work, and I continued to get worse. I remember sitting on our couch in the front room with my children next to me, silently crying out to God, *I don't have time for this; my children need me.*

That day, we felt led to go to a nearby church that we had never visited before. We had no idea of this beforehand, but as part of the service that day, the ministry team would be going through the aisles, praying for anyone who wanted to be healed. Hopeful that someone would come and pray for me, I stood up with my hands open. All of a sudden, without anyone touching me at all, Jesus Himself touched me in a powerful way. I was healed instantly. Brew, seeing the hand of God touching me, looked over at me with tears. We both started laughing and crying at the same time, as we stood there with our hands up to heaven, thanking God for His love and mercy. The pain and fever left right then and there. It was a miracle.

Soon after that, I woke up to half of my face paralyzed. Bell's palsy had struck me out of nowhere, and it stayed that way for six weeks.

While dealing with Bell's palsy, cataracts began to grow in both my eyes at a rapid pace. Though I was only 38 years old, my vision worsened daily to the point where I needed surgery on both eyes as soon as possible. The problem with that was we didn't have money for the surgeries and did not have insurance. Fortunately, God blessed us with a doctor who agreed to let us make payments on an $8,000 surgery with a $500 deposit. Brew's mom offered to help us with the down payment, and before my first surgery, I filled out the paperwork agreeing to the financial obligation. After both surgeries were completed, I got a call from the doctor's office saying that unfortunately for them, they could not find my financial agreement, which meant they couldn't charge me for my surgeries. They also informed me that they were sending the $500 deposit back to me and needed my address to do so.

I sat there on the other end of the phone in disbelief.

"What? Can you repeat that?"

She repeated everything to me again. I couldn't believe what I was hearing. The lady who was calling me and sharing this incredible news was dumbfounded as well. She said this had never happened before, told me to consider it a gift, and simply said goodbye. Another miracle! This time God healed my eyes through the hands of a surgeon and paid the bill.

During this physically challenging season, I prayed daily, asking God if we were to stay in Bend or head back to San Diego. We so longed to be with Nathan, but I was waiting and trusting God for His timing. I was weak, and we had a lot going on in Bend with two properties that God had blessed us with. Thank God, as Brew was praying about this decision, he felt clear that we were to go back to San Diego. Over the next few months, we excitedly started getting our affairs together to leave. We couldn't wait to get back home to be with our boy.

We arrived in San Diego in May of 2002. Being together again as a family was a huge celebration. Most of all, I felt tremendous relief. We were home.

A few months after being back, I woke up on the Saturday before Labor Day with my heart beating strangely and sporadically. My heart would race, then slow down and even stop for a few seconds, causing me to almost pass out. Then suddenly it would reboot with such force it felt like my heart was going to jump right out of my chest. I waited and prayed through the day, hoping it would go away by itself, but this continued all day and into the night.

We didn't have insurance. I knew if I went to the emergency room, it would be really expensive, but after a few hours, I got worried. Brew was out of town surfing with the kids for the weekend, so I called a friend to take me to the hospital that night. The doctors didn't know what was causing this, so they ended up keeping me in the heart clinic at the hospital for a week until I stabilized. By the end of the week, they still didn't know what the issue was, so they put me on a very strong drug and sent me home. I hated how the drug made me feel flatlined and not at all like myself.

After a couple months on the drug, I decided to go to a local healing service one evening to receive prayer for my heart. I shared with the people there who were praying that night what had happened and that I believed God was going to heal me. They laid hands on me and prayed, and I felt in my body that I had been healed. I took a step of faith and quit taking the medicine. That issue with my heart has never happened again, and that healing would mark the end of a long season of sickness.

We happily settled into living in San Diego. We were spending time with friends and enjoying the beach once again. Nathan, now in high school, was living with us again, and I was homeschooling Emily and Lily. Emily jumped right into a gymnastics program in San Diego, and Lily was starting to get into gymnastics too. Brew quickly got back to work as a landscape contractor and enjoyed reconnecting with all his old friends and surf buddies. I, too, was reconnecting with my friends in San Diego and was feeling happy and at peace. We were taking in international exchange students to help pay the rent and the kids loved having them in our home. It was a great season for our family.

In 2003, we decided to sell the first home we had bought in Bend, which made it possible to put money down on a house in San Diego. At the same time, God was speaking to me about getting my real estate license. I sadly let go of homeschooling and put the girls in the little public school at the end of our street. Once I got my real estate license, I started working right away. God blessed it, and I did really well. All the while, through the many changes, ups and downs, and twists and turns, God kept giving me visions about what was to come.

Chapter 12
It's Time

El Hanneman, The Faithful God

"Know therefore that the LORD your God is God; He is the faithful God, keeping His covenant of love to a thousand generations of those who love Him and keep His commandments."

—Deuteronomy 7:9

Adonai, Lord Master

"Sovereign LORD, you have begun to show to your servant your greatness and your strong hand. For what god is there in heaven or on earth who can do the deeds and mighty works you do?"

—Deuteronomy 3:24

"Behold I will do a new thing; now it shall spring forth, shall ye not know it? I will even make a way in the wilderness, and rivers in the desert."

—Isaiah 43:19 KJV

Soon, we started attending the church that we had been a part of for many years before moving to Bend. I began to go to a Tuesday morning bible study at this church, and on the second day I attended, a group of about seven women asked if they could pray for me at the end of the night. As they began to pray, God showed them those things I had been recording in my journals over the last five years. Though I hadn't shared these hopes and dreams with a single soul, the women began praying and speaking to me about what only God and I knew.

"I see a giant storehouse filled with things people need. Things you are able to provide," said one of the women. "I see that you will have great favor in the marketplace–that when you ask the rich for what is needed for the poor, they will give it to you." Another told me she saw a vision of a beautiful place that had a garden where people gathered, where children played, and where there was great joy and celebration. They also saw tables filled with food and plenty of toys, tools, and useful items–even roller skates!

With tears streaming down my face, I nodded *yes*. I was certain this was the confirmation of all the Lord had shown me. I had years of journals filled with pictures of this place and with words I had written that described exactly what they were seeing. That experience was the green light I needed to move forward. It was time to do this thing. What that meant exactly or how we were going to do that; I still didn't know.

I went home to tell my husband. "It's time," I said.

"Time for what?" Brew asked me.

I shared with him what was in my journals and what the women had seen in the Spirit at the Bible study and all they prayed for that day.

"How are we going to do this, Sheri?" he asked me.

"I don't know," I responded. "But we have been here before–trusting God in the unknown. We will trust Him again."

Soon, God led me to a woman who runs a non-profit called Momanna Ministries. She helped me come under her 501c3 umbrella to start my own organization. She was also a woman of faith and intercession and prayerfully supported me through the process.

In January 2005, we chose our name–Bridge of Hope. Our mission was to help women and children in transition by providing practical items needed to start over. That meant providing furniture and all household items. The hope was that providing these practical items and walking alongside these women in love and community would create a bridge that would help them up onto the other side of whatever they were facing. Bridge of Hope would minister to women in the same way I was ministered to as a single mom in need. God revealed His love and care for me and my son through what we now call, "the gospel of pots and pans," and that's what we were going to do for others.

I remember asking God, *Do I find the women first and then the stuff, or find the stuff and then the women who need it?*

He answered, *Don't worry about it.*

Another part of this vision was to create a place where people could be a part of something, where people could connect with others, serve, and use their gifts and talents. The Bible talks about every part of the body being important for the working of the whole body. Bridge of Hope would be a place for an individual to explore and grow in their unique giftings and be able to use their giftings without a lot of "red tape" or having to wait through twenty or more committee meetings to get approved.

In February of 2005, we officially stepped out and started Bridge of Hope. God clearly told me to remain faithful to study the Bible and to do one other thing. I was to study the life and ministry of George Mueller, the "Father of Orphans."

George Mueller simply believed in God and took Him at His word, including God's promises of provision. He believed that God would provide all that he needed practically and financially and started orphanages in England in the 1800s with nothing but prayer. He knew he wasn't supposed to start a campaign to raise funds or go from church to church asking for money. George spent time alone with God, reading the Bible, and asking only God, not other people, for what he needed for the orphans, for the orphanages, and for his personal needs. He would use his journals as part of his prayer time, recording the needs he was facing on the pages of his journal. He was just as faithful to record when the answer came in–the dollar amount right to the penny, along with the date the prayer was answered.

It struck me that George continually faced many challenging and demanding circumstances, which never let up throughout his life and ministry. But the same was true with the answers; they would always come. The requests became bigger and bigger, as God would call him to open more orphanages, which meant more children to feed and care for and more bills to pay. Eventually, he was opening up Bible colleges, continuing to trust God for every penny to come in for the schools as well. Another important fact I discovered was that the answers would usually come in at the last minute.

His faith moved me greatly, and I knew George was the example God was asking me to follow. George Mueller became my role model and mentor. I read everything I could about him and applied it to my own journey. As we began building Bridge of Hope, I did what George did. I began to write down in detail the financial needs of the ministry and other needs for both our family and Bridge of Hope.

Around the same time, a door opened for me to begin teaching a Bible study at a recovery home called Set Free San Diego. Just like the ministry we were a part of in Oregon, these women were coming in off the streets and into a structured program. Newly sober and meeting Jesus, they were finding freedom after being slaves to drugs and alcohol. Being a part of this ministry, I was able to connect with women who would be graduating and transitioning from Set Free and starting out on their own. This is where Bridge of Hope came in, as we were able to provide some furniture and other things that these mostly single mothers needed for their apartments. In our family's one-car garage, we would store furniture and other items that we found or someone would give us. After Brew finished work every day, I would take his truck to pick up furniture and deliver it to the women who needed it.

Taking on this task, we quickly outgrew our garage. We rented a room at the Baptist church on the corner by our house, which cost $400 a month–which by the way, we didn't have. So, we asked God to provide and signed the lease. The money miraculously came in every month for the year that we were there. Never a penny over. We continued to grow, waiting on God's provision and timing for everything. We would never push for more but followed His lead, connecting with one woman at a time, one day at a time.

Chapter 13
Springs in the Desert

El Shaddai, Almighty God

"When Abram was ninety-nine years old, the LORD appeared to him and said, 'I am God Almighty; walk before me and be blameless.'"

—Genesis 17:1

Elohei MaUzzi, God my Strong Fortress

"It is God who arms me with strength and keeps my way secure".
—Psalm 18:32

In 2006, the real estate market started to change negatively. Short sales and foreclosures were coming about. As a realtor, things were getting tougher and tougher. But as I prayed, I felt God reminding me of the Lord's prayer. "Give us this day our daily bread," Jesus said in Matthew 6:11 (NASB). God was showing me that He supplies what is needed for each day. If nothing happened, that *nothing* was the bread that He provided. If I had a deal, that was the bread He was providing, and I was meant to eat up! I trusted He knew what was best for me and my family, and He provided for the day, whether it looked like it to me or not.

On October 31, 2006, while I was at a breakfast meeting with a ministry we were partnering with, I got a call from Brew. When I got into my car, I sat and listened to his voicemail.

"Sheri, at the job this morning, something flew into my eye. It's not good. I am heading to the hospital."

I knew right away that if Brew was going to the hospital, it was serious. I started my car and drove as fast as I could to find him there, but he was already in surgery.

Brew had arrived on the job around 8:30 that morning and turned on his table saw to get it started. He was working on building a fence for his client. He hadn't started cutting the wood, so he hadn't put on his safety goggles yet but was simply getting ready to get started. Brew was looking towards the saw, standing 10 feet away, when suddenly a random thing happened. A piece of metal broke off the saw blade, shot straight through the air at incredible speed, and directly hit the middle of his left eye.

The doctors did emergency surgery to retrieve the quarter-inch piece of metal that had ripped up the interior of his eye, and thankfully, the piece of saw blade had just missed the optic nerve. His retina detached and the metal caused other serious damage to his eye, but the surgery to save his eye was a success. Before the surgery, we were told that he would most likely never see out of that eye again, but he could still see after the surgery. The doctor said Brew was her miracle man. However, the retina continued to pull away even after four more surgery attempts to attach it over the next seven months.

It was the toughest year of our life so far. This very hard-working, athletic, and active man couldn't do anything during his recovery. He couldn't even read. All he could do was sit. During this time, Brew's mother, who lived in Tennessee, was dying of cancer. Sadly, he was unable to travel above sea level because of his eye, so he couldn't even visit her to say goodbye. Brew was depressed for the first time in his life. Not only did he have to deal with a brain injury and his memory challenges every day, but now his vision was radically distorted and his depth perception gone. His life was changed forever.

In the midst of all of this, we were continuing to build Bridge of Hope, but now I was the sole provider. It was becoming clear why God had led me to real estate when He did because I was going to need to work and provide for our family. However, the market was starting to crash in 2007. Deals were falling through after months of hard work, and Brew and I were on the verge of going into debt just to pay for everyday expenses.

We were truly being tested to trust God in all things.

All the while, I continued to do what George Mueller did, which was to pray and seek Him for our daily needs. I stayed faithful to write down in detail all the financial needs for both our family and for Bridge of Hope. I would write the dollar amount needed on the left side of the paper, and when the answer came in, I would write it on the right side and date it.

During these really tough days, my prayer was always that we would be debt free and that we would be the head and not the tail; the one who can give and not the one to borrow. We prayed for our mortgage payment and for Bridge of Hope's rent every month. Many times, having nothing in the bank and no clue how it would come in, it would come on exactly the day it was needed. We prayed our property taxes in, money for bills to be paid, and deals to close. God would continually answer in a range of ways, ways that would bring me to my knees.

It was a difficult time, but I would not trade it for anything. Every day, we watched God do the impossible, bring in the funds, and provide answers. God provided us our daily bread, just enough for the day. This became the foundation of Bridge of Hope-to wait on the Lord for His timing and His provision. If we needed something-whether they were baby clothes, pots, pans, or furniture-we prayed and asked the Lord, and he would bring in those items. We witnessed daily that where God guides, He provides. If it is His will, it's His bill.

In April 2007, I had two real estate deals fall apart within days of closing, with nothing else in the pipeline. It was a devastating blow.

We were counting on that and needed the money badly. I continued to trust the Lord, but my heart was becoming weary with all Brew was going through and with my deals falling apart after months of hard work. Thankfully, my dearest friend Jackie gave us her cabin in Tahoe for a week to get away. While I was there, I was wrestling with God about what had just happened, and being the breadwinner, I was feeling the pressure of not having any deals on the horizon and no money in the bank.

Jesus, what am I to think, and where are You in all this?

As much as this was God's plan, to stretch and teach me to trust and be totally reliant on Him, I was getting tired. Every day, we would not know how the mortgage or something that the kids needed would be paid, but thank God, a refund check would show up out of nowhere, or a friend would be prompted by the Lord to send money or gift cards. It was truly exciting and exhausting all at the same time.

I put my journal down and went out to the front room to talk to Brew about it.

"If you had $20,000 in the bank right now, would you feel better?" he asked me.

"Yes, of course," I quickly responded.

"Why?" he asked me.

That struck me. *If I am a child of God, why would having money in the bank determine if I have peace or not? Why should that change anything? He is God, and if I have Him, I have everything.*

Brew's question brought a paradigm shift for me. I felt excited and ran into the back room to be alone with God and pray about this. I saw the truth once again. My Father God is my security, and He is faithful, even when I feel the most insecure. He is my provider even when I cannot see it. Money in the bank or not, He is my good Father. It's not about my comfort level.

As a matter of fact, I believe our comfort is not His priority. It's about Him and my trust in Him. I asked for forgiveness for complaining about the way He was providing. I confessed that I had gotten frustrated with the manna portions and how the provision was coming, instead of focusing on the fact that it *was* coming in! He was providing what we needed every day, and He never quit. We were being cared for by His daily bread, perfect for the day's needs. It was always enough.

I headed back to San Diego with a new outlook. I was finally understanding, in a whole new way, that our circumstances should not determine if we have peace or joy. Leaving Tahoe, we still didn't have any money in the bank, and there were no deals on the horizon, but I was excited about the future and about this new revelation.

Soon, I had one listing in a beautiful beach area called Del Mar. It was a little condo on the corner of a busy street right by the freeway–not a desirable location for many, but a great place to put up a sign and hopefully get some leads. I bought these cheap $4 signs and put them around the area, advertising the condo. Shortly after, I got a call from a man who saw one of my signs. He was going to be listing his house soon, which was in one of the most exclusive areas of San Diego, Del Mar Proper, and he wanted to talk to me about selling his house. I couldn't believe it because I was a nobody realtor in the area. We ended up having a great chat for about 20 minutes, and he told me that he'd like me to list his home and help him buy his next place. This was the biggest deal I had ever had up to that point. We had a buyer almost immediately for his home, who offered all cash. The house sold for just over $1 million in three weeks, and we purchased his new home for $650,000. After this, I had all the money I needed to pay back what I had to use on our equity line and had plenty left over. Plus, it all closed one week before Christmas, and we had the best Christmas ever that year.

This whole experience broke something loose in me. A greater faith was emerging. I began to hear that God would be leading me out of real estate in the next couple of years, and I would be full-time at Bridge of Hope. I had absolutely no idea how that would happen, but I wrote it down in my journal and prayed about it from time to time.

The metal blade and the piece that was in Brew's eye were tested and showed that the metal within the carbide tip was not properly bonded. We were in a good position for a settlement, and that was great news for us–so we decided to hire an attorney, ready for our next miracle.

Chapter 14
The Slanted Driveway

Yahweh Shammah, The LORD is there

"The distance all around will be 18,000 cubits. And the name of the city from that time on will be: THE LORD IS THERE."
—Ezekiel 48:35

Yahweh Osenu, The LORD our Maker

Come, let us bow down in worship, let us kneel before the LORD our Maker; for He is our God and we are the people of his pasture, the flock under His care.

—Psalm 95:6 -7

In the fall of 2007, we had outgrown the little room we were renting at the church and were looking for a bigger place for Bridge of Hope. As I prayed about this, I sensed the Holy Spirit impress upon me these words: *The city.* I did not know what that meant exactly because I felt like we were already in the city. But as I heard these words again and again in my spirit, I knew they were significant. I remember telling my husband that something new and exciting was about to happen. I could feel it.

Since the beginning of Bridge of Hope just two years prior, God had always provided just enough for our needs–our daily bread. We believed and often said out loud, "Where God guides, He provides" and "If it's His will, it's His bill." Then unexpectedly, we received a generous donation of $3,000 at the end of the year, an amount that far exceeded our financial responsibilities. We were so excited to see that much money come in. It felt like God gave us His stamp of approval, confirming we were on the right track. We now felt confident that God was leading us to a new place.

In fact, He was. I soon found a small shop for rent in the newspaper for $585 a month. It was in the city: City Heights, to be exact, a large urban community in the heart of San Diego.

At the time, I had no idea that this densely populated neighborhood of only 6.5 square miles held one of the largest refugee resettlement communities in the entire nation, where there are over 100 dialects spoken. I had no clue that City Heights, which was only 12 minutes south of my home, was a richly diverse community that celebrates multiple cultures . . . but God did.

The space that was for rent was perfect for us to be able to store more furniture and other donations. The property also had a gigantic tree out front, which towered over our driveway and provided lots of shade–a unique feature in a neighborhood crowded with mostly apartment buildings, mom and pop shops, and eateries serving cuisine from all around the world. The asking price was still over budget, however, so I decided to ask the owner to lower the price. Unfortunately, he wasn't willing to budge.

In the meantime, God began to get my attention in other ways. I just happened to pick up a newspaper with an article about a refugee boy from Uganda. He was living in City Heights and needed prosthetics due to a war injury in his homeland in Africa. My heart was struck by what I was reading. I wanted to know more, so I started to do research on refugees in San Diego, which led me right back to learning more about City Heights.

Then, over the course of five days, I was invited three times by three different people to a conference called *Jesus, Justice, and Poverty.*

Initially, I wasn't planning on going since I was just getting over the flu, but when the third invite came to me, I knew I was supposed to go. I cannot tell you exactly what was spoken at the conference, but I could feel God was doing something in my heart. Whenever I heard the words "City Heights," "refugees," or "immigrants" I would perk up. For many days following, I kept hearing the still small voice as described in the Bible repeating those words to me. I knew they were deeply significant in a way that was about to unfold.

Meanwhile, I continued to work, but the real estate market began to crash. Months of hard work amounted to nothing, with my deals falling through left and right. Brew also struggled, trying to adjust to his new and distorted vision, not to mention having to endure multiple surgeries that would continue through 2007. We pressed on through great adversity, believing God for His provision. The lawsuit continued with depositions, investigations, and very little hope that things would pan out as we needed. Despite everything, we continued to lay our burdens down to the Lord, believing and waiting on Him for every need, both in our personal lives and ministry.

After a couple months of Brew and I praying and waiting, the owner agreed to lower the price by fifty dollars a month. By faith, we signed the year lease on the building on 38th Street. We gave him the first month's rent but still needed another hundred dollars for the deposit. Once again, God came through. During our final walk-through on the property, we discovered a long copper pipe left in the building by the previous tenant. We quickly recycled it, bringing in $98 and change–making it possible to pay the deposit in full.

On November 7, 2007, we moved Bridge of Hope into our new building, not having a clue of the amazing adventure before us.

Our new building on 38th Street was nestled in a mostly residential area with a small Filipino restaurant across the street, the smell of fresh-ly cooked lumpia filling the air. We instantly felt at home in our new 900-square-foot shop with tall ceilings, a big roll-up garage door, and a slanted driveway. Word was starting to spread about Bridge of Hope, and some local churches and ministries wanted to know how they could help.

A couple of months after we moved in, we experienced what would become a significant turning point for Bridge of Hope. It was a sunny Saturday afternoon in January 2008 when I saw five beautiful children playing on the street next to our building and decided to walk over and say hello. They did not speak English, but we smiled a lot and did our best to communicate. Then, I had an idea. I had a couple of soccer balls in the shop, so I asked if they played soccer. They quickly responded "Yes!" with big smiles on their faces.

So, I walked them over to our property and opened the garage. As the door lifted and revealed all that was inside–furniture, household items, clothing, toys, and sports equipment –I could see wonder filling the eyes of these children, as if to say *This is all yours?* I saw the contents of our garage with fresh eyes, too. God had truly provided. With wide smiles, the kids pointed to a couple balls and looked at me for approval. "Go for it," I said, and the kids thanked me in their broken English, grabbed the balls, and rushed out. To my surprise, they returned to the shop after just a few minutes, this time with a couple adults and more children–an entire family. Brew and I welcomed them inside, and, gesturing with my hands, I told them, "If you need anything, please go ahead and take it!" So, this family of 14 began to look around and ask for a few pots and pans, socks, and a piece of furniture.

My husband leaned into me and whispered, "What's happening Sheri?"

I said, "I don't know, but it's happening . . . . so let's go with it!"

After a few minutes, I got a chance to talk with the father. I soon learned his name was Simon. Simon was originally from Uganda and spoke English pretty well. As we stood outside under the big shade tree, he told me how he had brought his family to America a few months before from a refugee camp in Kenya. Their story was one of great challenge and overcoming, and I was struck by their courage.

After about 10 minutes of talking to Simon, I grabbed a Bible from the shop and quickly ran back to him.

"Do you believe in Jesus, Simon?" I asked.

"Yes!" he responded with a big smile. I looked deeply into his warm and weary eyes for a few moments, aware of God knitting our hearts together. It felt like everything finally made sense.

"This is why we are here! We want to support you. We want to support the refugees."

Though I said this to Simon, I was really making a declaration to myself and to the world. I was putting a stake in the ground, and at that moment, Brew and I both sensed God's clear direction. Suddenly, I realized exactly what He had been doing over the past few months.

Simon looked at me, and I at him. With tears in our eyes, standing together on that slanted driveway, we both recognized that something significant was taking place. Holy ground. We didn't fully understand it, but we knew this had been a divinely planned encounter by the Almighty God.

The many refugees who have suffered great violence, injustice, pain, hunger, and sorrow were God's beautiful children. They were now here in San Diego, my new neighbors from all over the world. God was about to change my life forever in a powerful way, and He was going to do it through their stories. Through their stories of facing famine, warfare, terrorism, economic collapse, and life in a refugee camp. Through their faith, resilience, and love. I was the one who was receiving. I was the one who was learning more about Jesus and His love. It was me who was being awakened and changed.

By the following Saturday, Simon's whole family was waiting outside for me to arrive, and they had brought another Ugandan family with them, along with a few friends. I was both excited and nervous to see everybody. We greeted each other with handshakes, big smiles, and great anticipation for what the day would bring. I opened the garage door to the shop, and said, "Welcome! Come on in!"

We had an amazing day together, sharing what we had available and forming new friendships. Except for Simon, they only spoke Swahili, but somehow language was not an issue. Instead, we relied on smiles, laughter, and improvised sign language to communicate. It was the language of love, and it was beautiful and invigorating.

Within one month, I'd met about 100 new friends from Uganda, all of them with stories of surviving war with courage, strength, and love. They began to visit us on Saturday mornings, and we would exchange stories, laugh together, and of course, share our clothing and household items. I was inspired and encouraged, but this was only the beginning.

Word was out to the community about our garage on 38th. Soon, refugees and immigrants from all over the world were showing up on our driveway on Saturday morning. They would wait for me to open our doors and help them pick out household items, furniture, food, and provisions they desperately needed to make a new start in San Diego.

It wasn't just the stuff they were coming for, however. Bridge of Hope was a place to belong and feel safe. Our new friends needed a community and a place to meet others who were facing the same circumstances. They were seeking not only provision but connection. Ultimately, that's what it became about for Brew and me too–the friendships, the connections, the community.

One morning, our neighbor who lived next door walked over to the driveway after watching our visitors come and go for a few hours.

"Do you need help?" she asked me, sizing up how exhausted I must have looked after hauling around heavy goods and running up and down the driveway all morning.

I smiled. "No, I'm okay! But it's so nice to meet you."

She was unconvinced. "You do need help," she responded and walked right into the garage.

Boy, was she right. I soon learned my neighbor's name was Carolina. She was from Mexico, spoke fluent Spanish, and was gifted in administration. Soon, Carolina became my right hand every Saturday morning, helping to organize all of our possessions and stay on top of the clothing donations that were pouring in.

Every day, as I headed to our new Bridge of Hope location with a truck full of donations, I would pray that someone in the neighborhood would be available to help me unload the heavy furniture and other large items. And every day, I would pull up to the driveway, and neighbors would immediately run over and start unloading my truck and bringing things into the shop. I didn't even have to ask. Other times, they would see me sweeping and cleaning around the storehouse, and they would jump in and join me or take over what needed to be done. Those simple jobs were creating community in a way I had never experienced before.

A dear friend and sister in Christ, Kristine Chieh, had some time between jobs before going back to school to get her nursing degree. She told me she would visit Bridge of Hope for one week to help. That week turned into years of service, well after she got her degree and became a nurse. Kristine had a great mind for organizing and a huge heart of compassion. Together, she and I figured out how to create a system that could keep order and peace as more and more people were flooding in for hugs, love, fellowship, and basic necessities.

Six months after meeting Simon and his family, we had up to two hundred people at Bridge of Hope each Saturday morning. Families were bringing new families; even children were bringing new friends they had made in the neighborhood. It wouldn't matter if they had been enemies in their homeland or were from a place they'd never heard of before. If you were a refugee, another refugee would bring you to Bridge of Hope. Soon, our visitors joined in volunteering their own time, helping out with translation and manual tasks. They wanted to help other new arrivals and offered to translate for us and do anything that needed to be done. One particular blessing was a dear friend from Burundi, who spoke English and helped by interpreting in Swahili, which was greatly needed.

Before we'd start the day, the whole community would come together on the slanted driveway, hold hands, and pray together. We asked for God's blessing and protection on what the day would bring. We would pray in English, Spanish, Swahili, Napali, Arabic, and any other languages represented there that day.

We asked people from the community to help us translate and call out the names of visitors who signed up to come into the shop. Many of the names were almost impossible for me to read or pronounce. People were welcomed in, ten at a time, to visit the store and pick out clothing, kitchen items, furniture, and miscellaneous household supplies.

For everything that was going on there, it was a pretty small shop. Furniture was piled up on the right, and toys and books were stacked in the middle. Clothing and household items were lined up on the left. To be honest, the set-up was a bit precarious, and I would always pray before we started our day that a piece of furniture would not fall on anyone who would be in there.

Meanwhile, other visitors happily waited outside for their turn in the *storehouse,* as our garage was soon called. We put tables, chairs, and benches outside to make it comfortable for the adults, and even set up a foosball table on Saturday mornings for the kids. There was always a football or two being tossed from one side of the street to the other between cars passing, and my mom and daughters would often come with arts and crafts supplies to do projects with the kids (and sometimes, the adults too).

Through all of this, our neighbors showed us nothing but grace and patience. Our visitors often gathered on their driveways, sometimes as early as 3 AM, waiting for the day to begin. I would arrive on Saturday mornings around 7 AM, typically to find around a hundred people waiting outside. On my drive in, I would ask God to be with us, to protect the children, and to please help me with all the different languages that would be spoken to me (and all at the same time!)

I wanted so badly to be a conduit of God's love and care for each one, but in the process, my heavenly Father was also healing my own heart through the faith of my new friends. I heard about their homelands, their stories of war and genocide, and of course, their hopes and dreams for their futures in America. They had struggled, fought, and persevered through great pain and trauma, and maintained incredible hope and strength. Their faith that had been truly tested by fire challenged my own. Their love for culture and family–and the time they committed to both–impacted me greatly. Their joy in the simple things–not material things–shifted my perspective. Their gratitude for simply having arrived in America, and for having enough food, enough clothing, a safe place to live, and a place where their children could go to school often brought me to tears. Ultimately, the refugees and immigrants who had come to San Diego looking for a better life would become not only my sisters, brothers, and dearest friends; they would become my teachers.

It was powerful, beautiful, and holy, every bit of it.

Chapter 15
A Thriving Bridge

Miqweh Yisrael, Hope for Israel

Blessed is the man who trusts in the LORD, And whose trust is the LORD. For he shall be like a tree planted by the waters, which spreads out its roots by the river, and will not fear when heat comes; But its leaf will be green, and will not be anxious in the year of drought, Nor will cease from yielding fruit.

—Jeremiah 17:7-8 NKJV

El Tamim, Perfect God

"He is the Rock, his works are perfect, and all His ways are just. A faithful God who does no wrong, upright and just is He."

—Deuteronomy 32:4

In 2009, I felt God speak to me about learning to provide food for people. After all, the Bible does tell us to feed the hungry.

"And if you offer yourself to the hungry and satisfy the need of the afflicted, Then your light will rise in the darkness. And your gloom will become like midday."

—(Isaiah 58:10) NASB

Ironically, not many people cheered me on in my pursuit. Even fellow Christians warned me that it was a huge undertaking, that it would be impossible. But I knew God was leading me in this direction, and I began reaching out to the local food banks and grocery stores to see if they could help me get started.

I even decided to take a trip up to the Dream Center in Los Angeles to see how they run their food program and neighborhood distributions. I showed up on a weekday, thinking I was going to take a formal class, but instead, a staff member put me on a box crate in the back of a food truck filled with hundreds of pounds of produce. We were headed to a sidewalk in downtown Los Angeles to do a food distribution to the homeless and others in need. As we flew down the LA freeway trying to get to our destination on time, I was excited, encouraged, and a little frightened. I thought, *we could do this!*

My experience with the Dream Center showed me that we don't have to figure everything out to answer the call of God. We just have to say yes.

Bridge of Hope soon began to partner with the local food banks where Brew and I would go every Thursday morning to gather produce. One by one, we stacked boxes of apples, oranges, onions, and potatoes in the back of our truck. On Saturday mornings, we would set up a table in front of our building and put out the produce for people to take home.

Soon, more people began coming on Saturday mornings to pick up free produce, pantry items, and packaged food. We began to gather more food from the food banks. I even began to get calls from strangers who had heard about what we were doing and wanted to connect us to bakeries and other food sources. It was amazing to see how God was providing every week. It was just one more confirmation that "Where God guides, He provides."

During this time, I got a call from a friend who was also a volunteer.

"By any chance, could you use a van?" he asked me.

I laughed. Could we use a van? Absolutely.

It turns out that his company was letting go of some of their cargo vans. These vans had low mileage and had been meticulously maintained, but they weren't useful anymore for the company. Soon, we had a van that was perfect for transporting food and a growing demand of supplies.

As we continued to grow, we stayed faithful to wait on God for every penny and for every need. He blessed us with a couple of incredible connections. One was with a consignment clothing store, which provided bags of beautiful clothes every Monday. The other was a local furniture outlet, which came as a miraculous answer to prayer. We had been in great need of beds, so we did what we always did (and still do): we prayed and asked God specifically for beds.

Later that week, I got a call from a furniture store in Los Angeles. Though I had never heard of them before, they knew about us. The manager proceeded to tell me that they were clearing out a bunch of their inventory and asked if we needed beds.

I gave them an enthusiastic "Yes!" but then explained that we weren't able to drive up to Los Angeles. "No worries," he responded, and told us that they would be sending down a truck that day piled high with sixteen brand-new beds.

I fell to my knees in tears, in complete awe of the goodness of God for His people.

College groups from Intervarsity and couples from my church were soon regularly committing to spend time with the kids and help us with manual work and chores at Bridge of Hope. We did not have a formal sign on the building, just a poster board saying "Welcome." It also had a few rules we learned we needed, along with the hours we were open to the public.

As we were growing and needed more space, we bought an old utility truck that became our food pantry. When we weren't using it to pick up furniture, it sat on our driveway and became extra space for us to store food. About ten women from the community faithfully volunteered to pack up the food we'd collected throughout the week and load it onto the truck to prepare for Saturday mornings.

In one year, we went from serving about 20 families to over 200 families a week.

When we would open our doors on Saturday morning, the whole community would participate. The children couldn't wait to help us set up the tables and chairs and carry out the foosball table and art supplies. Of course, they would always include a football to toss back and forth across the street. The local teens would put themselves on a rotation of who was going to work in the store that day. The adults worked hard at sorting goods and managing operations.

There was always a lot of excitement in the air–a sense of anticipation and celebration for what and who the day would bring.

Saturday mornings were giving us all a sense of awareness that we were a part of something bigger. People were coming together. Walls of separation were coming down. Prejudices were being destroyed. Children from all parts of the world played together, as their parents watched and made new friends themselves. Different cultures and backgrounds blended together on one tiny driveway. It was beautiful not only to us but to God.

It was a simple thing that brought us together and showed us that we are all the same. It was provision. I never felt that I had anything more to offer than my experience of how I had been cared for and helped by God. I wanted others to experience the meticulous care that He has for all of us. I wanted them to see it is God, the perfect Parent, who provides and cares for His people.

One of the beautiful things that started to happen as a result of coming together was that people began helping each other. It was as if a key had been used to open a door of "love thy neighbor as thyself" (Matthew 22:39). People began to see the needs of their neighbors and new arrivals and began to bring things from home to share with others. Children were doing this as well, becoming shepherds of each other and looking out for newcomers. Initially, I did not understand the tribal differences and old bitterness that affected some of the people we were serving. I once overheard that "if Sheri can give to others who are different from herself, we can too." That blew me away. I never would have thought that through this simple time together each week, God was breaking down fears, barriers, and divisions rooted in a decades-old conflict in entirely different countries.

In the meanwhile, my family's life was forever changed. We were making new friends every day, even being invited into people's homes to share a meal. Despite the language barrier, we would end up sharing deep belly laughs–and sometimes tears–and praying together. We continually witnessed God pouring in everything we needed every day. We just kept saying, "Yes" to Him. Not only did we pray in finances and donations, but we prayed in volunteers as well. If they had to move on, we would pray for the person who would be joining us soon. He would always bring someone for the next season of what was needed.

Rain or shine, we were there on the sidewalk every Saturday. One rainy weekend before Thanksgiving, we put up a tarp, suspending it between the building and the truck to keep people from getting wet. Right before we were ending the day, a friend of mine called and asked if we wanted a Thanksgiving meal. She had attended a big event and was given all the leftover turkey, mashed potatoes, stuffing, green beans, and pie. She said it was still warm and enough for fifty people, which was about how many were still there. Of course, I agreed, so she jumped in her car and quickly drove it down to Bridge of Hope. That ended up being one of the sweetest and most memorable Thanksgiving meals ever. There we were, huddled together under a tarp on the slanted driveway, enjoying a feast.

One day, some of my Ugandan friends and I were on the driveway going through the boxes of newly donated clothing when we saw a man walking toward Bridge of Hope. He had tears in his eyes and was obviously struggling. I asked him if we could pray for him, and without any hesitation, he fell to his knees on our driveway. As he raised his hands up to heaven, we laid our hands on Him and prayed for healing and for freedom from addiction. God was clearly calling him to come home.

We learned that this man's name was Virgil and that he was homeless and living behind a nearby building. Soon after meeting Virgil, whenever he would see me pull up with a truckload, he was there to help. I felt God tell me to allow him to help, even though he was still in the depths of a serious addiction. Using or not, he belonged there, and God loved Him and had a plan for his life.

Over the next couple of years, Virgil went in and out of the hospital due to his drug use and congestive heart failure. Finally, he committed himself to the Rescue Mission for one year, re-dedicated his life to the Lord, and began a life of sobriety. God immediately blessed him with a pacemaker and a new life. Soon, Virgil came back to Bridge of Hope after graduating from the program and worked with me every day. He went from sleeping outside, using crack cocaine for years, and almost dying numerous times, to being trusted with the keys to our building and our vehicles. He was even voted deacon of the year at his church.

Around this time, I began to notice a group of kids in the neighborhood ranging in age from about one year old to 13. They would often be walking around by themselves, pushing a baby in a stroller without any parents or adults in sight. One day, I started up a conversation with the kids, gave them something to eat, and learned their stories. They were from two different families, both squatting in an abandoned duplex with no running water or electricity. They would come by a few days a week to chat and to ask me for something to eat and for clothing, underwear, and whatever else they needed. One of the children shared that their mom was in prison, but their dad was present–though he evidently wasn't parenting his five kids. They seemed to love and fear their father, who was part of a gang.

One morning, the kids came to Bridge of Hope cold, hungry and tired. I got down on my knees so I could look them in the eyes and share Jesus with them. They were really listening and had good questions for me. I asked if they wanted to know Jesus and invite him into their hearts. One by one, they said yes. Right there on the slanted driveway, we prayed together, and Jesus filled their beautiful, broken hearts.

From then on, I knew it was my responsibility to teach them God's Word and to disciple them. Every Wednesday, I would walk a few blocks to their school, pick up the children–and usually, a few of their friends–and we would all walk to the park for our little Bible club. We would play games, memorize scripture, and act out the Bible stories we were learning about. It was a wonderful, sweet time with the kids. One beautiful Sunday afternoon, Brew and I were blessed with the awesome privilege of baptizing all thirteen children in a friend's pool.

A dear friend of mine wanted children badly but was unable to have her own. One Saturday, she came down to Bridge of Hope to do arts and crafts with the kids in the neighborhood and met five of these children. Someone had recently given her tickets to the circus, so we reached out to their father to ask if she could take them that evening. Happy to let her take them for the night, she packed the kids into her car, and they had a wonderful evening at the circus. But at the end of the night, their father was nowhere to be found and not answering his phone. While the kids sat in her car, she waited outside their duplex, calling him until almost midnight. Finally, he picked up the phone and told my friend to keep them. If she didn't take them home, they were going to be taken to Polinsky Center–a county holding place for children waiting to be placed in foster care.

My friend had only wanted to take the kids to the circus for the evening, but now she was faced with bringing them all home. She sat there in her car in the middle of the night in a dangerous part of the city, completely baffled and heartbroken for these precious children. Their father was willing to send them away.

Long story short, my dear friend brought all five children home that night. She was open to whatever God was doing and felt blessed to have them with her. She and her husband waited on God as He opened doors for each of the kids to move into safe living situations. However, she and her husband kept the baby and were blessed to be able to adopt her some years later. Another incredible miracle and answer to prayer.

We stayed in that building on 38th Street for five years. We had almost 100 salvations occur on the driveway, many of which were led by a dear friend of mine who would show up every Saturday morning. She would simply introduce herself and without hesitation, invite people to meet Jesus, and they would! That led to a Spanish-speaking Bible study held in the upstairs apartment we rented above our storehouse. In those five years, we established many strong and wonderful relationships with local principals, pastors, and store owners. God brought folks from other parts of San Diego to put on large events for our families in the park at the end of 38th Street. We held dinners, barbecues, parties, and celebrations for hundreds of people throughout the years. A beautiful community was evolving with love and grace at the center of it all.

After five years on 38th Street, we had outgrown our space. It was time to look for a bigger place. We had about 100 children and youth with us every week, and we no longer had the space to host youth groups or kid's clubs. We wanted to be good stewards of this amazing blessing and privilege, and the children and youth needed mentors, teachers, and tutors. In addition to that, we had long outgrown that space in terms of storage and inventory.

But again, we did not do anything without waiting for the Lord's leading. We visited quite a few buildings in the area, but they were way out of our price range and didn't fit with the vision the Lord had shown me. Intentional to never overstep His plan or pace, we were patient. We knew by our experience thus far and by the word of God, that His yoke is easy and His burden is light. And so, we waited.

Chapter 16
New Digs

Rishon Ve-Akharon, Alpha and Omega, First and Last

"Listen to me, Jacob, Israel, whom I have called: I am He; am the first and I am the last. My own hand laid the foundations of the earth, and my right hand spread out the heavens; when I summon them, they all stand up together."

—Isaiah 48:12- 13

El Olam, Everlasting God

"Do you not know? Have you not heard? The LORD is the everlasting God, the creator of the ends of the earth. He will not grow tired or weary, and His understanding no one can fathom. He gives strength to the weary and increases power to the weak".

—Isaiah 40: 28-29

One Sunday, I was resting on the couch, and I heard that still small voice saying, "Open Craigslist and go to the rental section."

I didn't hesitate, jumped right on the computer, and went to the rental section. An interesting-looking place had just been listed less than thirty minutes before I got online. It was an old building that was three times the size of ours on a 10,000-square-foot lot. It was listed for $1500 per month and only about ten blocks from where we already were. It was a rare property that you just don't see in City Heights, with enough room for the children to play safely away from the street, and big enough for us to do what we do.

The building was listed in *dilapidated condition,* which sounded like an opportunity to us.

I called the number on the ad right away and made an appointment to meet the owner the next day. When we got there, it looked like a broken-down, abandoned building on nothing but dirt surrounded by a barbed wire fence. It was in *really* bad shape, but the size of the space and location was perfect. We could see that with a lot of hard work, it could be just what we need for our growing ministry.

We were already used to paying the amount of rent needed. The stretching of our faith this time was that the property needed a ton of work just to be habitable and safe. I was concerned about how our small team could get this building where it needed to be in a short amount of time. Brew, being a full-time landscape contractor, couldn't give much time, and this was a job for not just one, but many professionals. We needed plumbers, electricians, framers, drywallers, and painters.

The Lord would have to bring the laborers, finances, materials, contractors, and more to make this work.

Walking inside the building felt like a maze. There were broken windows, torn-out walls, holes in the ceilings, floors ripped out, feral cats, and large families of pigeons living inside with all their poop. Thankfully, Brew could see past all the work that needed to be done and knew we needed to go for it. We signed the lease, and the landlord gave us three months of free rent. As a matter of fact, instead of us giving him a deposit, he gave us $4,000 towards replacing the roof that had leaks everywhere. The fact that the landlord gave us money just to lease the property was a huge confirmation.

A wonderful couple on our board are contractors. The Alleways came down and did a walk-through of the building and asked me, "What do you want?" What do you need?" I thought they were just asking me what I hoped to see one day. I drew out what our ideal design would be for this building to be functional for providing furniture, household items, clothing, and food.

They looked at the design and said, "Just tell us what you want, and we will do it."

I asked them to clarify. Unbelievably, they were offering to do the work for free. Along with their team, they came in and did about $30,000 worth of work, pro bono, to create what that building is today. They separated out departments and sectioned off parts of the building for greater efficiency and flow. They installed new electrical, plumbing, toilets, water heater, walls, ceilings, windows, and doors. They even found a staircase that leads to the upstairs that was hidden behind a wall. A wonderful painting contractor blessed us with all the paint. Another painting contractor helped Brew paint the entire building. But before the paint went on the walls, dear friends of mine who love Bridge of Hope wrote scriptures on the walls throughout the building. People were reaching out and wanted to come and clean the yard and do what was needed to get Bridge of Hope ready for the community.

It was coming together above and beyond all we could ask or think possible. We said goodbye to 38th Street and moved over to Fairmount Ave, the land of plenty.

There was plenty of space to play, be organized, and plant a garden: a dwelling place for the Lord and His kids to gather. Another huge blessing that came along was a donation of 21 fruit trees for our property from Dryers Ice Cream.

We continued to put our roots down in our new neighborhood. Bridge of Hope was booming, and it was definitely time for more help.

At the beginning of 2012, God brought two amazing women to Bridge of Hope at the same time and just in time: Cecelia Brito and Tammy Mason.

More and more Individuals, churches, and organizations began to hear about us and come. Word continued to go out, and God would bring connections, people, supplies, and all that was needed week after week.

We were now known throughout San Diego County. Agencies, caseworkers, individuals, churches, and local organizations were referring families in transition to us every week. We were welcoming at least 40 new refugee families a month into our Bridge of Hope family. We were supplying furniture, household items, clothing, and food to hundreds every month.

We had a booming youth group of refugee youth, kid's clubs, Bible studies, visiting missions teams, and a church called Puente de Vida, led by our beloved Cuco and Robyn Moya and the World Impact team. It was incredible, beautiful, wild, and very much alive.

We continued to stay in the posture of praying in every penny and waiting on God. We prayed for *all* the needs of the ministry. God continued to provide. Not only did He provide; He provided abundantly.

Brew's court case was still pending. The attorney on the other side was *extremely* difficult. He wasn't budging on our offer to settle, and what they were offering wasn't even enough to cover Brew's medical bills thus far, which already amounted to hundreds of thousands of dollars. We continued to pray and trust the Lord through the bad reports we'd hear from our attorney. We desperately needed a financial breakthrough. About a year and a half after we opened the case, our attorney called and told us that the attorney on the other side had been taken off the case. We were able to make a deal with the new attorney and the case was settled.

Brew's medical bills were paid in full, and we were able to pay back the debt incurred by our living expenses with more left over. I could now be in full-time ministry and not work in real estate any longer, which was what the Lord had spoken a year prior. Specific prayers were answered once again, including my request that we would be debt free.

Seven miraculous and extraordinarily challenging years after Bridge of Hope had begun, we experienced a breakthrough. Seven–the number of completion. I'm sad that my husband has had to go through what he has experienced. His eyesight is very difficult for him to live with every day. Brew is the most resilient person I know, who never complains and continues pressing on through many difficulties. He's continued to work hard, even though he's had many excuses not to over the years. This accident ended up blessing the work of our hands, and we were able to continue with what God has laid before us to do.

In 2011, we experienced another financial miracle. The interest rate on our home loan was soon to adjust, and it seemed impossible for us to keep the house and pay the mortgage each month. I continued to hold this before the Lord in prayer and felt He was going to make a way, but I didn't have a clue how.

One morning I woke to a strange voicemail left by a woman I had never met before. She had met my mother a couple times and had known about Bridge of Hope, but that's it. Her voice message said something like this, "You're going to think this is weird, but God woke me up in the early morning hours and asked me to turn on the television, watch, write down what I hear, and tell Sheri Briggs about it." It was one of those long infomercials that play around 2:00 a.m. about a non-profit that helps people who have had a crisis to get a loan modification so they don't lose their homes. I listened as she explained everything and the details of where the event will be held, their website, and what to bring to the event which was only a week away. She said that I needed to go. It was a bit strange, but the Lord had impressed on my heart a couple of months earlier that He would make a way for us to keep the house. He gave me the sense that I had to get everything in order on my end, and He would do it.

She called a second time, pleading with me to go. She even went down the list on my voice message, telling me every document I needed to bring to the event, just in case I hadn't checked out the website yet. She also added what I need to bring for lunch because it was going to be a long day. After that second call from her, I agreed to go. Brew did too, with his shoebox of business receipts in hand. We got there at 7:00 AM and stayed until 7:00 PM. At the end of the day, we were told that we were eligible for a modification. There was hope for us to keep our home.

But that was just where the hard work began. It took about six months in total to get the modification, and I will never forget the day when we finally heard the news. Brew and I were at Bridge of Hope doing some yard work when we got the call. Half of what we owed on our equity line, which was what we lived on during Brew's recovery, was, and the first mortgage interest rate was dropped to 1.5%. We could stay in our home and afford to do so.

In fact, we were now going to be paying a few hundred dollars less than what we had been paying for the last 10 years. Once again, God answered our prayers in a mighty way.

"But those who wait on the LORD shall renew their strength; They shall mount up with wings like eagles, They shall run and not be weary, They shall walk and not faint." Isaiah 40:31 NKJV

Thank God for that amazing woman I didn't know, who listened to the Holy Spirit, persisted through the fear of sounding strange, and called me twice to make sure I got the message, encouraging me to go. God does this stuff. He loves His kids and speaks to them.

At this same time, God began to bring in more financial support to Bridge of Hope. We actually had money in the account, and it was growing. God was preparing us for miracle after miracle, evidence of His faithfulness and goodness in our lives and in the lives of our community members.

(Note: To read more about how God moved at Bridge of Hope from 2010-2015, go to the Appendix).

Chapter 17
Adopted by ABBA

"For you have not received a spirit of slavery leading to fear again, but you have received a spirit of adoption as sons and daughters by which we cry out, 'Abba! Father!'"

—Romans 8:15 NASB

El Yashuati, God is my Salvation

"Guide me in Your truth, and teach me, for You are the God of my salvation. I wait for You all day long."

—Psalm 25:5 NHEB

In September 2012, I went to a conference in Los Angeles where a missionary named Heidi Baker was speaking for three days. It was wonderful, but the greatest times for me were the times between the conference hours when I was alone with God in my hotel room. The last year had been incredible. I had experienced so much of God's amazing grace and miraculous love. But still, something was missing. I felt a longing in my heart, and the only way I knew how to describe it was a deep loneliness.

In those hours between sessions, I would meet with my heavenly Father, asking him questions and encountering Him. But it wasn't until the last day that I got a breakthrough.

The last hour before I was to check out, I sat in my room and cried out to Him, *"What is it, Lord?" I don't want to leave without whatever it is I need from you. Show me, Lord!*

I heard His still, small voice say something that changed me forever.

I am adopting you. You are my child, not your father's child. You are mine.

I not only heard these words crystal-clear; I felt them to the very core of my body. They weren't just words. It was as if a verdict had been announced.

I heard Him again.

I have adopted you.

He said it as if He was the judge in a courtroom, slamming the gavel down.

You are my daughter.

It was a complete paradigm shift for me. The Bible says that "*all who are led by the Spirit of God are children of God,*" and that, "*The Spirit you receive does not make you slaves, so that you live in fear again; rather, the Spirit you received brought about your adoption to sonship. And by Him we cry, 'Abba, Father.'*" (Romans 8: 14,15). It says that "*As a father has compassion on his children, so the Lord has compassion on those who fear him*" (Psalm 103:13).

I knew all these scriptures, and many more, on adoption, sonship, and God as a Father.

But at that moment, I understood them differently. These beliefs had lived in my head, and not my heart. Knowing I was God's daughter, that He had adopted me, *me*–changed everything. I realized that before that point, I had believed myself to be an orphan, rather than a truly loved child of God. This was the missing piece that would change everything.

I was so excited that I started saying out loud, "Father? Papa, you adopted me? Am I really yours?"

Again, in the stillness of my heart, He made His response clear to me. *The adoption papers were signed by my Son's blood. It is done, finished, finalized, and nothing can ever change that.*

At this point, there were only a few minutes before check-out time. I had to pack up quickly and get out of there, but I didn't want to leave. I wanted to keep talking to my heavenly Father about this revelation and soak in the beauty and wonder of it all. I heard Him say, *Let's go get some ice cream.*

Ice cream? I asked.

I began to think in my head, *I don't want ice cream. I haven't even had breakfast yet.* But I caught myself and thought, *Wait a minute. My dad is asking me to get ice cream with Him. Of course, I want to go!* I hurriedly got my things together and quickly left the hotel, jumped in my car, and began driving to find an ice cream shop. I found a 31 Flavors right on the coast, so I parked my truck and went in. I hadn't been in an ice cream shop for a long time. I felt giddy, like a little kid, and ordered my old favorite–chocolate and peanut butter. I heard the Lord's voice say, *Don't get back in your truck. Let's sit here on this bench and look at the ocean together.*

This was the beginning of a beautiful new relationship with my Papa God. I was 47 years old when this miracle happened. Looking back now, I see how loving and tender the timing of this was. God wanted to establish the truth of Him adopting me and the depth of what that means for me before I was to head into deeper healing that I desperately needed–healing from my complicated and abusive relationship with my earthly father.

Just one year later, I was driving up to Los Angeles to visit my daughter for the day at Biola University. On the drive up, I was feeling overwhelmed. That deep emptiness was creeping up again. Something wasn't right, even though I had just been adopted and there was so much life, beauty, and wonder I was experiencing. I was a mother to amazing children, and I experienced tremendous love and joy every day with my family and my Bridge of Hope community. But I could feel that there was shame and something deeply painful inside of me.

So, right there on the freeway, I asked the Holy Spirit to show me if there was anything I needed to know or understand. *God, what is causing this feeling?*

I heard the Holy Spirit gently ask me, *Are you ready to go here?*

It felt like I was standing on the edge of a rocky 100-foot cliff. It was my turn to jump, but I was afraid I wouldn't land in the right spot. I was afraid I wouldn't make it out alive. Still, I said, *Yes.*

With tears welling up in my eyes, I got off the freeway at the next exit and sat in my truck on the side of the road. As I closed my eyes, I was taken to what seemed like a scene from a movie. As if I was watching from the seats in a movie theater, the Holy Spirit showed me something that had happened frequently as I was growing up. He asked me to sit, stay, and watch it from the eyes of a mother. Replay; now watch it from the eyes of my own children. Replay; last time, now watch it from the eyes of a spouse. I was shocked at what I was experiencing, which felt like the first time I was seeing this. I broke down sobbing, feeling the terror of it all, as I watched these scenes play out. My Papa God sat with me, holding me close. I began to cry in a way I never had before. The sounds coming up from my belly didn't sound human. Deep grief, too deep for words. Pain, fear, heartbreak, and travail, all at the same time. He sat with me and held me as I agreed to stay and not run, feeling the horrific pain, facing the truth, and determined not to deny or minimize what had happened. I remained there, held by the One who adopted me.

The reality of what life was like for me as a child shook me to my core. I chose to step into it and accept what had happened, right there on the side of the road. This experience was only the tip of the iceberg. What was underneath was unknown at that point. God was about to untangle me; break lies off of me that I didn't know I was carrying and that I've lived under my entire life. He was bringing in the light to shine on the dark corners of my soul. He was teaching me the love, purity, and safety of a real Father. My radical Savior was about to untie and set straight what real love is and what it is not.

"Yea, though I walk through the valley of the shadow of death, I will fear no evil: for thou art with me…," says Psalm 23:4 (KJV). I had to go back to that valley with Him and face my past, so He could give me the truth. He was going to heal the little girl inside me, the one who had taken on mindsets and survival skills for how to stay safe. Those decisions

that served me as a child were now destructive to me as an adult. God was starting the process of setting my mind and heart straight. He was beginning the work of dismantling, piece by piece, story by story, the faulty programming that shadowed my existence. He was giving me the truth that would eventually set me free.

As He began this work in me, right there off the 5 Freeway, I asked Him, *Are you sure now is a good time to do this? It feels like bad timing with so much going on right now with Bridge of Hope and my family.* But I knew there was no turning back. No matter how busy it felt, this was the time and season to begin this difficult journey into my childhood.

God led me to wise, godly counsel and to safe and loving people to help me, catch me, and walk with me through this painful valley. I stayed the course, working through and acknowledging the many layers of abuse. I continue to do this work. My hope is to comfort others, as my Papa God has truly comforted me.

One thing I have learned is that God uses us in our brokenness. If He had to wait to completely heal us before we were ready for the work we are called to do, it would never happen. He uses us as we go along. He changes us, refines us, and rebuilds us, as we are in motion. His gifts are irrevocable no matter what has happened or hasn't happened yet.

As a matter of fact, recognizing and embracing our brokenness gives us the ability to understand and empathize with other's brokenness. She who is forgiven much loves much, which means He redeems it all. He can take what is broken and make it whole. We are never disqualified because of our past, but when we surrender to Him and His kingdom, we go from glory to glory in this journey called life.

> *" . . . in all things God works for the good of those who love him, who have been called according to his purpose."*
> —Romans 8:28

Chapter 18
Nathan

Yahweh Bashamayim, God in Heaven

"Acknowledge and take to heart this day that the LORD is God in heaven above and on the earth below. There is no other."
—Deuteronomy 4:39

Elohei Mikkarov, God who is near

"'Am I a God who is near,' declares the LORD, 'And not a God far off?'"
—Jeremiah 23:23 NASB

This will be the hardest chapter to write. I am trembling as I begin to try to put my broken heart into words.

June 2015–all was well. Both Brew and I were working hard and feeling blessed by God's care for our family, and His continual provision for Bridge of Hope. My children were all doing fantastic. Sean was living with his mom in Washington and beginning a new career in construction. Eric was living in La Jolla, working at a great job he'd had for the last five years and continuing his education in IT to become a videographer. Emily had just graduated from Biola University with a degree in Business Marketing. She was super excited for her future and already had job opportunities ahead of her. Lily was just finishing up her first year at Parsons in New York City. She is an amazingly gifted artist and loved the city and all it had to offer.

My son Nathan was living the beautiful life he created for himself; traveling, surfing, diving, always surrounding himself with friends, and making new friends everywhere he went, both young and old. He was hardworking and adventurous. He loved to explore, always ready for the next big adventure. He was passionate about good food, music, nature, and the simple things in life. He was smart, kind, genuine, and warmhearted–a gatherer, a lover, a unique and authentic soul.

My precious son Nathan Adams Upton died on June 3, 2015, in a free diving accident in Mexico, in Agua Verde–*the green water.*

The last time we spoke before he headed down to Mexico for a 10-day trip, he told me, "Mom, when I get back, I want to take you out to dinner."

I said, "I would love that. I can't wait! Have fun and be safe. I love you."

"I love you too, Mom!"

It was a busy Wednesday at Bridge of Hope. Looking back now, it felt like the entire day was set up like scenes in a play. I remember feeling quite aware of the people around me, showing their love and care for me in ways that stood out to me. Especially around the time when my son was drowning in the green water, 20 hours south in Baja. At 1 PM a dear friend, who had just returned from her home country of Iraq, brought me gifts and greetings from her family. At 2 PM, right around the time Nathan passed away, I was invited to have a fish lunch at the home of a family newly arrived from Burundi. Thinking back on those moments, it's striking to me that my son died catching a fish at the same time I was eating one.

After my fish lunch and time with the family, I decided to make one last stop before heading home. A hotel in La Jolla was donating a lot of beautiful bedding to Bridge of Hope: hundreds of down comforters and practically new high-end sheets and pillows. For us, that was hitting the jackpot. It was a sweet day.

At 10 PM, just before we got into bed, my son Eric called and asked to speak to his dad. I told him he was asleep. He asked me to wake him and said that he needed to talk to him. It sounded serious, so I woke Brew up and gave him the phone. Brew got out of bed and told me that Eric was outside of our house. I thought, *Wow, something is really bothering him. He came all the way up here this late to talk to his dad and doesn't even want to come in the house.* Brew put on his shoes and went outside to see what was up. My thought was, *that Eric broke up with his girlfriend and is in deep distress.* I began to pray that God would give Brew the right words and asked God to comfort Eric's broken heart.

Five minutes later, Brew came back into the house and stood in the doorway.

"Sheri, I need to talk to you."

"Is Eric okay?"

"Yes," he said. "It's not Eric."

This got my attention. I looked up at Brew, and there was silence between us for a few moments as Brew searched for words.

"It's Nathan."

"What about Nathan?" I said, trying to sound lighthearted.

He hesitated to answer and looked around the room.

"What about Nathan?"

Never, not once, for a single second would I ever have imagined the words that I was about to hear. It was not even a possibility or a consideration in my mind for one moment of my entire life.

"He was diving, and he didn't make it. He drowned . . . Nathan died."

From there, all went black.

A force deep inside my mother's body threw me off the bed. *No! No!*

I crumbled to the ground and rose back up again, violently thrashing myself through the hallway and in and out of rooms, beating the walls that surrounded me. The sounds and screams that came out of me were not human. The woman, the mother who carried and nursed this beautiful child, began to convulse and break. *No! No! No! I was on the floor, pounding on the ground and screaming, I do not want to be this woman! I want my son! I want my Nathan! It's not time. I need more time.*

Lily had just returned home from New York for summer break. She woke up to my screams and the terror echoing through our small home and came running out of her room.

"Mom! What's wrong?"

I screamed at the top of my lungs, 'Nathan is dead!" Lily collapsed to the ground and began to wail.

Emily was in Newport Beach, where she was living at the time. Lily called and told her the horrific news that their dear brother was gone, and sadly, Emily was alone when she heard the unfathomable. Brew asked her not to drive by herself that night, bearing all the pain alone, so she drove home early the next morning. After a couple hours of hell, I called my mom to tell her and then my brother, begging him to come as quickly as he could.

Around 1 AM, I called my best friend Jackie, waking her in the middle of the night to tell her that my precious son was dead.

Nathan was an avid waterman: an excellent surfer, diver, swimmer, and fisherman who had spent all of his 26 years in the water. He had been to Agua Verde several times before with friends and over the years had spent lots of time fishing there with his dad. It's a long drive from San Diego, about 20 hours, and the trip to the green water is long and dangerous with narrow rocky roads over treacherous thousand-foot cliffs. But once you arrive, it is breathtakingly beautiful–a serene island surrounded by aqua blue water and tiny islands.

Nathan and his friends had been so excited about this trip. Their plan was to go spearfishing during the day and camp on the beach at night, enjoying sashimi and fish tacos from the day's catch for dinner. Nathan's childhood friend Pat, Pat's girlfriend Maria, who was also a dear friend of Nate's, and Nathan's girlfriend Madison, got up early the next day after arriving and looked for a *ponga*, a small fishing boat, that would take them out to the islands to go diving for the day. They had high hopes to catch lots of *pargo*, red snapper. Nate's friend Pat was a certified diver and a lifeguard. He was catching fish that day, but Nate wasn't having as much success, which was unusual for him. He wanted to go down one last time, and this time, he was sure he would catch something. It was about 2 PM when Nate loaded his gun and jumped into the water. The story that has been told to me is that he dove down for a few minutes and came back up excited about a 50-pound pargo that he had just seen. He eagerly reloaded his spear gun, and with a big smile and great anticipation of catching this big fish, he dove down into the beautiful green water.

He never came back up.

Pat and the girls were swimming close by when the ponga driver yelled, "Something is wrong with your friend." Pat saw Nate's gun floating on the surface of the water, and they all began to panic, swimming around and searching for Nathan. Pat dove down. It was an unusually clear day, one like the locals hadn't seen in years, and Pat could see 66 feet down, where Nathan lay face up at the bottom of the green water. He came up for air, taking in a deep breath and trying with everything in him to hold onto his senses and regulate his breathing so that he could go back down and get his friend.

Nathan and Pat had been best friends since they were 13 years old. The trauma and fear running through his body made it impossible to hold his breath long enough to get to Nathan. He tried to regulate his breathing and dove down again, doing everything he could to contain himself and rescue his closest friend. He'd get close but would have to come back up to catch his breath and try again. He dove and dove, over and over, but could not do it without almost dying himself. He tried and tried, but blood began to come out of his ears and eyes. At this point, too much time had passed. He had to stop. Nathan was gone.

They radioed into the Federalis, begging for help to get Nathan out of the water. Word came back that the Federalis were coming, but hours passed, and nobody came to his rescue. Nathan's friends watched and waited in the 110-degree heat as their dear friend lay alone at the bottom of the Sea of Cortez.

Time was passing, and it was imperative that they get Nathan out of the water before dark. They stayed anchored above his body. Pat had $300 cash with him. He got back on the radio, crying out for help, "Anybody out there! Please help! Does anybody want to make $300? Please come with tanks! My friend has drowned, and we need to get him out." They had been waiting for about four hours at that point when somebody came within the hour of Pat offering money. Nathan was pulled up out of the water and placed in the boat, where his swollen body lay next to his friends.

I cannot imagine what those precious ones had to endure that day. Unthinkable trauma has placed a mark on their hearts and minds forever. The helplessness of seeing their dear friend die, lying at the bottom of the ocean. Having to endure hours of fear and terror, living a nightmare, not knowing how they would get Nathan out of the water.

As the ponga driver headed for shore, they held each other in the back of the boat. Their beloved friend's body was there, but he was gone. When they arrived, the locals were gathered on the beach, waiting for their return. Once on shore, people surrounded them, caring for them and Nathan. Each of the kids called their parents to tell them the horrible news. Pat's dad and other close friends of Nathan immediately jumped on planes that night and headed to Agua Verde to be with the kids and bring Nathan's truck, which he had just purchased and was so excited about, back to San Diego.

On the night of Nathan's passing, Nathan's dad had just arrived in Constitution, only a couple hours south of Agua Verde. The plan was that they would drive down to meet him there the next day. The fact that Nate's dad was in Mexico at the time Nathan died turned out to be vital for all that had to happen to get our son home.

No one knew how to reach Terry to tell him what had happened. After searching through Nathan's house, Eric found a phone number on his refrigerator that appeared to be from Mexico. Brew called it, and thank God, it was Andres, Terry's good friend, with whom he was staying for the night in Baja. Andres, his wife Kika, and their children were all like family to Nathan, who had spent a lot of time with them since he was a child. Kika answered the call that night and handed the phone to Terry. Brew broke the news to him that his only son was gone.

Again, there are no words to describe these moments and the days and months to follow.

The next morning at daybreak, Terry, Andres, and Junior, Andres' son who was one of Nathan's dearest friends, drove to the hospital in Loretto. They identified Nathan's body and began planning to get him home as soon as possible. My heart breaks for Nathan's father to have had to see his son in those horrific moments and to have to work so hard under such stress to get his son out of Mexico and home to all of us. I am beyond thankful for him and his strength to do the impossible.

Meanwhile, I could hardly speak. I could not think. I was sick. I was in shock. My precious daughter Emily arrived the next morning, completely shattered, but somehow able to take over for us. She handled all the communication and planning with Nathan's dad, the Mexican consulate, and three different mortuaries. Two were in Mexico, Loretto and Tijuana, and one in San Diego.

Being in a community of cultures where death and grieving were done differently, I had become aware that I could have my son brought directly to our home instead of a mortuary. When Terry asked me what I wanted to do, there was no question in my mind.

"Bring him home. Just get him home!"

"Okay. It will happen." I knew he would do it. He was the feet on the ground in Mexico, and he made everything happen that needed to . . . coordinating with the hospital, mortuary, and the government. By God's grace and under Terry's guidance, everything came together. The mortuary that cared for our son dressed him nicely, placed his body in a casket, and got him on the airplane, which safely arrived in Tijuana on Saturday, June 6–three days after his death. Terry boarded a plane and headed back to San Diego, right behind his son.

After three long, horrific days of waiting, I will never forget those last couple hours before his return. There we were, all of us sitting in the house, waiting for word that he made it into the U.S. My hands gripped the couch beneath me until my fingers were stuck, my mind in a vacuum, my body numb from pain, adrenaline pumping at the same time. All of us with broken and ravaged hearts, waiting. The call came through at 3 PM telling us, "Nathan has arrived. He is here on American soil."

Relief.

My boy was coming home for the last time.

At 3:30 PM, Nate's dad arrived. When he walked into my house, we embraced, holding onto each other and sobbing. Our son was gone. My dear friends had been working and preparing our home for his arrival. Food and flowers poured in, and a few gathered to make Lily's old art studio in our backyard a place for Nathan while he was with us. They brought in candles and created a beautiful space for him to rest and for us to gather around him.

When the black hearse arrived at 4 PM that Saturday, there are no words to describe what that was like–relief that he was home, fear of the unknown, knowing, but not believing that my son was dead. *He's here, but it's not him anymore. What will I see? What will I do when I see him?* They brought the casket through the side yard, passing right by where I was sitting and waiting. Brew directed them into the room that was prepared for him. His dad warned me about seeing him because of the time that had passed since he died and the hot weather conditions in Mexico. Not to mention, Nathan had been in the water for a long time.

I desperately wanted to see him.

Terry went in first to see if everything was okay for me to go in. He waved to me from across the yard that it was alright and that it was time for me to be with my son.

I walked into the room. At first glance, I had to quickly catch my breath and steady myself. That was not my Nathan. But I quickly looked past what I couldn't bear, so that I could be fully present with him. I walked towards his gorgeous thick, curly hair, the hair that I have loved, and run my fingers through his entire life. I pulled my chair close to his head and looked from the top of him down to his feet, which were covered. Apparently, his feet were changing faster than the other parts of him. That was hard for me. I really wanted to see them, but Terry told me it wasn't a good idea.

I sat with my boy. I stayed there and did not leave his side.

I stroked Nathan's hair for a long time. I talked to him. I felt peace sitting and touching him, keeping one hand on him the entire time. I told him how much I loved him and how proud I was of him. I prayed. I cried. I sat with my son. I loved every minute of being with him. I eventually moved my chair closer to the top portion of his body, looking at all of him and feeling completely comfortable. I would walk around the room, go in and out and talk to him, no longer seeing that he didn't look like my Nate.

After about an hour alone with Nathan, Eric, Emily, and Lily had a moment with him, but it was too difficult for them to stay. We also invited his close friends, of which there were many. We wanted them to have time with Nathan and have a chance to say goodbye to their beloved friend and brother.

His friends and our family friends gathered together, around 100 in total, and stayed up all night and into the early morning. A few would come in at a time as I sat with my son. They shared stories of how Nathan had impacted their lives. He loved others so well, and for that fact, I am most proud. This experience continued all through the night, and I did not want to leave him for a second because I knew my time was short. I did go to sleep for a couple hours around 3:00 AM but woke as the sun came up and ran out to be with my son for the few final hours. I wanted as much time as possible before they would come to take him away forever.

Terry and I sat with Nathan together for about an hour that morning. It was both a beautiful and deeply sorrowful time for us. I cannot explain these moments. God was with us, and Nathan was with God, and we were all together under the shadow of His wing.

In these worst moments of my life, I felt the profoundly tangible presence of God, sitting between us and all around us, as we sat as close to our son as we possibly could.

In 1988, we so joyously welcomed our beloved child, who was born at home, into this world. We said our goodbyes to him at home, and I am so pleased with those decisions. The angels surrounded us at his birth, celebrating this beautiful new life that would change our lives forever. Now, the angels surrounded us as they welcomed him into his new home, and again, our lives were changed forever.

Around 10 AM that next morning, the driver from the mortuary came. It was time.

I watched as they closed the casket, rolled him out of the room, moved him back through the side yard, and out to the street where the hearse was parked and waiting. They loaded him in, closed the door, and started to drive away with my son. I walked behind the hearse that had my beloved child inside, and out into the middle of the street, where I stood alone watching until I couldn't see him any longer.

My beautiful child was gone. This heavenly gift, that taught me love and to trust God with everything I had, was now with the One who gave him to me. Who would've thought this child was on loan to me? Who would've thought this love would have so much sorrow?

My best friend Jackie coordinated the entire memorial service and handled many details and conversations that needed attention. There are no words to describe my gratitude and thankfulness for what she did for me and my family. My dear friends and community from Bridge of Hope came and helped out with the planning and cared for me, my family, and my home. People from all around the community placed candles around Bridge of Hope in honor of my son. My friends from all over the world came to see me and bring their culture and the ways they have honored the valley of death in their homelands. In the darkest hours of my soul, they weren't afraid to be with me.

We had a beautiful service where over 500 people came to honor my beloved son. God gave me the strength to speak at the service and to speak clearly, sharing all that was on my heart to honor my son. There was also a wake, where Nathan's ashes were scattered at Windansea Beach in La Jolla. As I sat in the boat past the waves, I watched as hundreds of surfers, including my husband and children, jumped on their boards and paddled towards me, holding red roses in their mouths and waiting to release Nate's ashes into the water. It was an incredible sight and hard to express what that looked and felt like as I watched them all coming toward me. Once they arrived at the boat, they formed a circle. My mom, my best friend Jackie, my sister-in-law, and my niece stayed with me on the boat. There are no words to describe these moments of love and terror. This was it, the final moment to say goodbye. I tried to take in every second, every look, every tear, and every word spoken out on the water that day. Once they were there, Nathan's dad took the ashes and poured them into the water with a loud cry. The surfers looked up to the heavens and began yelling to Nathan," We love you, Nate!" throwing their roses in the air, "We love you, Nathan! See you on the other side!"

It was beautiful and terrible all at the same time.

Nathan was dearly loved and respected by many; both young and old were in the water that day. It was a very proud moment for this mother. My son, deeply loved, cherished, and known by hundreds of people, made a huge impact on the souls of many. Nathan had many circles of friends, and he brought people together that would have never known each other unless Nathan had introduced them. He saw people. They mattered to him. He enjoyed life and its fullness. In his brief 26 years of living, he taught us what living and loving well means. He's an exceptional human being with a heart of gold.

As I write this, it has been four and a half years since I saw his beautiful face or heard his voice.

Nathan and the blessing of being Nate's mom were the inspiration behind Bridge of Hope. His name and legacy live on not only there, but in all the communities he touched both here and around the globe.

Chapter 19
Life after Loss

Yahweh Shalom, The LORD is my Peace

"But the LORD said to him, 'Peace! Do not be afraid. You are not going to die.' So Gideon built an altar to the LORD there and called it The LORD is Peace..."

—Judges 6:23- 24

Yahweh Rohi, The LORD is my Shepherd

"Yea, though I walk through the valley of the shadow of death, I will fear no evil, for you are with me. Your rod and Your staff comfort me."

—Psalms 23:4 NKJV

I'll never have the right words to fully describe my journey forward after Nate passed.

But I'll do what I can–I'll share stories.

After losing Nathan, I was completely broken. I not only lost my son but I lost myself. I felt betrayed by my God. I struggled with the fact that my Father knew I could never bear this. *How could my loving heavenly Father let this happen? The One who adopted me and promised to protect me all the days of my life? How?* I had promises from God for my son and for our family that I had been holding onto for years. I trusted Him with my son. I prayed for Nate's safety every day since before he was born. At the time of his passing, we had been in a beautiful season of experiencing that unique time when children grow up and draw close to their families again.

Despair, deep sadness, and loneliness filled my entire being. My theology was shaken. Where was I to go? The One who had been my safe place and refuge didn't feel safe anymore. I wanted to hide in Him like I always had, but I felt betrayed by Him. The unthinkable had happened. As a result, I lost all I believed to be sure and true.

Another part of me felt like my innocence was stolen. The worst possible thing had happened, so now I was living with new fears. *What nightmare could happen next? Would I lose another child? What tragedy lays waiting for me?* Somewhere along the path of my Christian walk, my theology subconsciously told me that losing a child could never happen to me. But now, I became aware that the unthinkable could happen.

What now?

I was aware of God's tender presence, standing near, giving me all the space and grace, I needed in this desert wasteland. But I had been radically assaulted by death. God made women to be protectors, givers of life, those who would die for their children. There was no map for this new reality in my body or brain. It was against the very DNA that God gave me: to give birth and to protect and raise a child. Hosea 13:8 says, "Like a bear robbed of her cubs, I will attack them and rip them open . . ." Made in His image, I am also fierce and fearless for my children. How would the reality of what happened and the truth of Scripture be reconciled in this broken soul? Nathan's death went against everything I am and was made to be.

But in His tender love and compassion, God was not threatened by my distance and confusion. Instead, He remained close, waiting for me. When I did come to Him in prayer, I felt orphaned. I didn't know how to get inside His presence, and I wasn't even sure if I wanted to be there anymore. My unspoken and unconscious beliefs about what life is supposed to look like were shaken and brought to the surface when Nathan died. This was a radical reality check. I learned that I am not immune to devastation.

> *"Though He slay me, yet I will trust Him…"*
> —Job 15:13 KJV

A year and a half after Nathan passed away, I went away to a house in Mexico for four days. I needed to be alone, which is something I've needed a lot of since Nathan died. I was hurting and angry, reminding God that He created me to be a mother–one who loves and protects her children, not bury them. My child dying went against every fiber of my being. It felt, in short, impossible. I needed time in silence and solitude to walk and journal. But by the last day, I still hadn't heard anything that brought me comfort. I was desperate for answers and relief, *something* that could help me go on.

One word! God, I need to hear you.

Suddenly, an hour before I was to go, I heard in that still, small voice, *I have compassion for you. I see you.*

I stopped, stunned. I had heard something.

He said it again.

I have compassion for you. I see you.

I was instantly undone by His empathy and the deep sadness I felt He had for me. I said out loud, feeling a glimmer of hope, "I believe you."

I began repeating back the words out loud, "He sees me. He has compassion for me." I then heard, "I am stopping for you."

In those moments, I felt something different for the first time since my son had died. *He sees me.* My deep pain and loss felt validated by His presence, His compassion. He was with me in the room. I sat there on the couch, feeling His words and presence holding me still. There was so much peace. Our relationship was restored at that moment. I felt safe again with my Father. I needed Him. I needed to bury myself under His wings (Psalm 91:4). From that moment forward, I understood that I wasn't alone in my pain, but we were *together* in the darkest hour of my soul. He was with me in my despair, feeling every pang that I did. He is the One who can handle my grief, where others can't. The light of dawn had broken through. I found my true comforter, my Papa, and felt safe once again.

I decided to go on a walk, repeating the words back to Him, *I have compassion for you. I see you.* I looked up to see a hawk circling above me. He would circle over a pasture to the left of me, then back to hover over me, then back to the pasture and all around me. I heard my Father say, *Look at the hawk. Look how he is circling over the land, watching everything beneath him, carefully surveying and watching. I am like the hawk. I am watching you and will watch out for you and will never take my eyes off of you. I'm hovering over you, continually surveying the land around you. I see you.*

"Lord, if this is really you speaking to me," I said out loud, "please have this hawk stay with me on this entire two-mile hike." The hawk stayed, circling above me the whole time until my walk was over and I went back into the house. God spoke to me through His creation that day, just like His word says He does.

When a friend of mine came to pick me up and bring me back to San Diego, I couldn't wait to share with him the words God spoke to me and about the hawk. He told me that the hawk is known as the *seer.* That was another beautiful confirmation of God's word to me, "I see you."

About three years after losing my son, I went away to be alone with God again and pray about something that felt unresolved and confusing to me.

Do you remember when Nathan's dad wanted to keep him during Christmas break and not send him back home to Oregon? How I prayed and sought the Lord, and He spoke specifically through a stranger in a little church, answering my cry to know God's will for Nathan? Well, I had questions.

So, I went up to the treehouse to be alone with Jesus. This was a place in my own backyard, a place I have been blessed with throughout my grief journey. I sat on the couch, looking at the trees outside blowing in the wind, as I sat crying out to God. *What was that all about? I surrendered my son to you in faith, believing I would have him with me all the days of my life. You said he was going to walk with you. I trusted You, and I let him go. I gave him up for a time I was hoping for and counting on. I lost that time with Nathan, and I can never get it back.*

Instantly, a picture came to my mind. I saw myself on one side of God and Nathan on the other. I felt God cradle me under one arm, and Nathan was huddled under the other. Our Father God was sitting in between us. He encouraged me to say everything to Nathan that I needed and wanted to say. My heart exploded. I was undone as I poured my words and heart out to my precious boy, holding nothing back. I sobbed about all my regrets about the lost time, the lost opportunities to be with him while he was alive. I heard the Lord say those same words spoken to me in the tiny chapel in Oregon. *You will always be his mama.*

Then I had one singular impression: I am known in Heaven as "Nathan's mama." I heard it like it was a name reserved for me forever–Nathan's mama. When those words were spoken to me in Oregon all those years before, this is not the meaning I imagined. But still, they were true–I would be his mama for eternity.

In African culture, they take the name of the first-born child and put it with mama or papa, and that is the parent's name and identity in their community. In an African community, I would be known as "Mama Nathan." That name would always be true. It was spoken to me that day in a tiny yellow chapel in Oregon, which comforted me when I was asked to let him go to live with his dad. Those same words bring me comfort today, as I have had to let him go to live with His Dad in Heaven.

I am and will always be Nathan's mama.

But there was another question I had for God. I was struggling with the fact that my son's life was obviously spared in our car crash, but God chose not to save him in Agua Verde. Omniscient and omnipresent, God was obviously capable of saving Nathan. Why didn't he do it the second time around?

The Lord showed me that if my son had died in our car crash, I would have never been able to forgive myself. Nathan didn't have his seatbelt on. My precious Jesus protected him and kept him alive and well that Memorial Day of 1999 and blessed this mother with the miracle of his life being spared. I got 14 more years with him. That tormenting thought is now a place of thankfulness and gratitude.

My son died doing what he loves to do in his favorite place in the world. He was gently and lovingly scooped up from the bottom of the sea and embraced by Jesus in the peace and quiet of the green waters.

"The Lord is near to the broken hearted and saves those who are crushed in Spirit."
—Psalm 34:18 NASB

He has never been more near.

"Blessed are those who mourn, for they shall be comforted."
—Matthew 5:4 NKJV

It is true.

God has clearly held each of my children's broken hearts as they grieve and long to have their brother with them. But they continue on by God's grace. After Nathan died, one of his friends made a T-shirt with a picture of him surfing that says, "Live Like Nate." My children have embraced this to the fullest. His life, his love for others, his love for adventure, travel, and different cultures have challenged them to want to live like Nate.

Emily is a successful videographer and has her own business called Narrative Films. She is very creative and loves what she does. She can travel and tell stories through film, and her work is changing lives. A year after Nathan died, she headed out on an adventure through Thailand, Bali, the Maldives, Australia, and New Zealand; all the places Nathan wanted to go. Today, Emily lives by the ocean and is enjoying surfing, diving, camping, enjoying time with her friends, and living life in a big way.

Lily came home after completing a year and a half at Parsons in New York. After losing her brother, we encouraged her to come back to San Diego to restore her heart and body. She came home and discovered a positive way to help her continue moving forward with a broken heart. She began to work out and started teaching kickboxing classes. That led her to get her certification to become a personal trainer, and she started a very successful business of her own. She also went back to school to become an esthetician. She not only created a business in fitness and skincare but uses her artistic skills as a make-up artist and is loving it.

Eric saved his money and planned a trip to Southeast Asia. He wanted to travel, film, and teach himself videography. He also chose to live like Nate and see the world, choosing a path for his profession that would bring him life. He had countless wonderful experiences on his travels and has grown to be an incredible videographer as well. His company is called Borrego Studios. "Borrego" is Nathan's nickname, given to him years ago by his closest friends.

We don't get to see Sean as much as we would like, but he has found a great passion and talent in building and construction, just like his dad. He is living and working in Washington state.

I am so proud of them all. They have forged paths to not only survive but thrive. They are carrying their brother's legacy so beautifully, stepping into who they really are and what they want from this life. It amazes and blesses me. They also carry wisdom in their young years that only grief can give, which has come with a great cost.

Brew continues to work with tenacity and resilience. He always has worked and has pressed on through many injuries and obstacles with a very positive attitude. It has been an incredible example to us all. No matter what has happened that day or what difficulty he faces with his poor vision and memory challenges, He praises God–and it's real. He picks up his guitar after a long day and worships His Lord. He lives out the words, ". . . If God is for us, who can be against us?" Romans 8:31

Thanks to God and all the amazing volunteers and supporters, Bridge of Hope continues to serve many people from all backgrounds and circumstances, week after week. The community is always welcome to come for food and clothing each week, and we receive referrals from over 70 different agencies in San Diego that work with a variety of people in different circumstances. We are here. We do what we do and are prepared and ready for whatever comes our way.

Personally, I am a different person since losing my son. It has been four years since Nathan died. They say when you lose a child, it is like walking around without skin on. I couldn't agree more. As time goes on, the pain and sorrow don't leave because the love is as alive as it was the day he was born. However, the familiarity of the pain is part of me. It's my new skin, day in and day out; it's familiar to me now. I know this cloak. Deep emptiness and brokenness have brought me closer to my Heavenly Father. For that, I am truly grateful. My vision was forced to change to see that walking with Him doesn't mean the terrible can't happen. It doesn't guarantee a neat and tidy life. It doesn't mean all your dreams will manifest just the way you want them to. This was my expectation about life and God that I didn't even know I had until my son was taken from me. They were unspoken beliefs that were shaken and brought to the surface when he died.

The richness of my Father God, this life, and the relationships He has surrounded me with are all the more real and appreciated. Nature, with its sounds and beauty, never ceases to captivate me. Things that perish don't have a hold on me any longer. I am thankful for that. I've slowed down. I see things differently. I see the beauty of suffering and the depths of where God takes us in suffering. I am not afraid of the darkness or going into another's dark and broken place. That too, I am grateful for.

"Though I walk through the valley of the shadow of death, I fear no evil for Thou art with me."
—Psalm 23:4 KJV

As long as I am on this earth, I will not have an answer as to why this happened. Many people have wanted to tell me why this happened and how I should be thinking, feeling, and experiencing the death of my son. When I was a single mother, people couldn't wait to give their opinions and advice on what I should and should not do. But I know without a doubt, that there is only one voice that can comfort us, guide us, and give us peace in the unknown darkness and mysteries of this life, and that is our Father God.

I know I will see my son again. I have been blessed to have this assurance. I cannot wait, and I dream of the day when I can hold his face, look him in the eyes, and hug my precious son.

When Nathan was born, the gift of his life changed mine forever, teaching me love and what is real and true. The gift of his death has forever changed my life, teaching me love and what is real and true.

For the rest of my days, I hope to be a comfort to others the way I've been comforted. At Bridge of Hope, we are surrounded by those who have suffered greatly due to war and other traumas and losses. Many mothers from other parts of the world have greatly comforted me in my grief in ways I cannot put into words. Many didn't speak English to me in my brokenness but just stood in silence, holding their heart, not afraid to look into my eyes as their tears fell. I hope to carry that same understanding to those who are suffering around me.

I have been blessed while on this treacherous road. I have not been forsaken. I have a greater understanding of grief, the Comforter, and the need for safe places to heal after loss and trauma. God willing, I want to bring that awareness in a more intentional way to others.

It's been 17 years since Bridge of Hope began. We have stayed true to waiting on God to guide and provide. I continue to record both ministry and personal needs in my journals and to record the answers as they come in. Knowing more now, I see why God led us this way. We did not have money to start this ministry, even to pay our own personal bills. God was requiring us to seek Him for every penny, and we have seen His faithfulness over and over again.

I hope this book has encouraged you to believe in who God is and put to practice what the Bible says. Step out where He is leading you. It is possible to have a working faith. Life is never without pain or suffering, times of lack, and times of plenty, but He is an unchanging God, who never leaves us or forsakes us. He alone is faithful.

Conclusion:
Yahweh is the ultimate perfect Father

Recently, I felt the Holy Spirit gave me a picture of myself lying face down on a huge rock; my whole body completely spread out, clinging to this rock. I knew this was a picture to remind me that God is our rock. He is Immovable, unchanging, always there, always loving, and always faithful. *He is the only thing that cannot be moved.* I was reminded of the scripture in Matthew 24:35, "Heaven and earth will pass away, but my words will never pass away.". This world is constantly changing- wars, rumors of war, suffering, pain, sorrow, death, and dying…. Yet, He is the rock that does not change or grow weary or pull away. Yahweh is guaranteed security. His character, nature, and attributes don't change. He is no respecter of persons, but He remains the same toward all his creation. We can trust in every name that describes Him. We can run and hide in His name that is above every name.

You may say, "Why then do bad things happen? If He is a loving God, why is there so much suffering? Why did He not answer my prayers the way I was believing Him to?"

We live in a broken world, but He is not of this world, and we are told as believers, we too are not of this world.

As we walk on the earth and through the valleys of death, He is with us. He is our immovable, unchanging God who is with us and never leaves. In Him, we find refuge in the darkest hours of our souls.

He is all His name promises to us. Even before a suicide, He is unchanging love. Before an overdose, He is unchanging love and all the names that describe Him. Even in a car crash, or cancer, no matter what the situation or how tragic or evil, He is unchanging love. His mercy, nearness, and beauty doesn't leave. He cannot abandon who He is. Many will walk away or turn their heads, but He stays.

"'Though the mountains be shaken and the hills be removed, yet my unfailing love for you will not be shaken nor my covenant of peace be removed,' says the LORD, who has compassion on you." Isaiah 54:10

Let go and fall into the hands of your beloved. The One who will never fail you, even in the darkest hours of your soul and the darkest hours this world has known His light and His love will never end.

My encouragement to you is to be in His Word. Feast on His Word. Study His names and anchor yourself on the truth of who God is. Press into Him. Spend time with your Father God. There is always more that He has for you; a deeper relationship with Him is waiting for you.

He desires to have a deep and intimate relationship with each one of us and fill us with the Holy Spirit. We are called to be a city on a hill, where we shine His love, light, and truth to this dark world.

You might only have a few loaves and a couple fish, but by faith, offer it up to Him and watch Him multiply it for the nations. Surrender all you are. I promise you, you will not be disappointed.

Acknowledgments:

Thank you to my beautiful son Nathan.
You've taught me so much and your legacy lives
on in all you touched.
You are forever loved and missed.
I cannot wait to see you in heaven and hold you
again my beloved child.

Thank you to my amazing daughters Emily and Lily, who have blessed my life beyond belief. Thank you for loving me, believing in me, and supporting me. There has been a cost, and I could not have done any of it without your love and your support. You both bring so much joy into my life and you inspire me every day!

Thank you, Brew, for your willingness to work so hard over the years: landscaping, picking up furniture, fixing things, building things, loving people, and loving me.

Thank you to my best friend Jackie who has been with me since our boys met when they were five. You have been such a beautiful, faithful friend who is always there for me. You have taught me what true friendship really is. I love you, my dear and faithful friend!

Thank you, Mom, for loving me and for your commitment to pray!

Thank you, Jimmy, for being a great brother and friend to me.

Thank you to all the behind-the-scene prayer warriors who have continued each week to hold me and Bridge of Hope up in prayer over the years: Jackie, Mom, Cindy, Sheila, Emebet, Tammy, and the Zellers. I am sure there are more, so thank you, too. There are no words to express my gratitude.

Thank you to all my dear friends that have come alongside me, loved me, and walked with me.

Thank you to all our Bridge of Hope donors and supporters that have blessed and provided for Bridge of Hope all these years. Thank you for trusting us. We could not have done any of this without you.

I want to say a special thank you to the Pike family for blessing Bridge of Hope and me personally over the years. Thank you for caring for me and my family. Thank you for your abundant love and generosity.

Thank you to all the amazing, faithful volunteers, who have served at Bridge of Hope through the years. You are the reason we have been so successful. You are the bridge of HOPE. We are a family, and you have been my family in ways you will never know. I love you ALL!!!

Thank you to all our partners in this work, who have provided and blessed Bridge of Hope over the years: Flood Church, Gracepoint Church, Venture Church, All People's Church, Maker's Church, Grace Church, Pomerado Church, Coast Vineyard, National Charity League Teen Volunteers in Action, Feeding San Diego, San Diego Food Bank, Trader Joes, City of Refuge, World Impact San Diego, and Father's House Church.

Thank you to all those who have blessed and supported the Nathan Upton Scholarship Award. You are changing lives!

I want to say thank you to all my amazing friends who have loved me and stood by me in my time of grief. You have been there for me, loving me, crying with me, and holding me up. Thank you.

ACKNOWLEDGMENTS:

Thank you to my community who has welcomed and embraced me.

Thank you, Laurie and Van, for giving me a place to go over and over again. You have no idea how you have blessed me.

Thank you, Sheri and Brad, for your love and friendship and for giving me a place to go in Mexico when I have needed it.

Thank you, Cece, for being a rock for this organization. Thank you for your leadership and for stepping in with so much love for the community.

Thank you, Randy and Renee Kay, for trusting me and giving me an opportunity to share my heart and support those who are grieving.

Thank you, Bob and Lauren Hasson, for encouraging me over the years with prophetic words, and to write this book!

Thank you, Eric and Sean, for accepting me into your life and loving me.

Thank you, Kelsey Smith, for your encouragement and for helping me with my book. I could not have done this without you. Thank you for being a wonderful editor and friend.

Thank you most of all, my Papa God, for loving me. For never leaving me. For cheering me on. For giving me your presence and teaching me how much you love me. You are my hero. May my footsteps follow Your way until everything in me brings honor to Your name.

Appendix
Testimonies and Journal Entries

Yahweh Jireh, The LORD who provides

"So Abraham called that place The LORD Will Provide. And to this day it is said, 'On the mountain of the LORD it will be provided.'"

—Genesis 22:14

El Haggadol, The Great God

"For the LORD your God is God of gods and Lord of lords, the great God, mighty and awesome, who shows no partiality and accepts no bribes."

—Deuteronomy 10:17

Sunday came, and still no money for rent. I was worshiping God at church, trying to focus on Him and not the rent, when I felt a tap on my shoulder. The person behind me handed me a check and whispered in my ear, "I can't believe how much God is asking me to give you." I turned around and opened the check. It was the total amount of rent due!

I began to cry with my hands up to heaven, "Thank you, Jesus! You are amazing!" At that moment, I had a very clear and beautiful vision that God gave me about this journey. I saw a picture of me as a little girl, pigtails in my hair, and wearing the crocheted pink dress my precious grandma had made me when I was five years old. I was holding onto the giant hand of my heavenly Father, walking next to me. My arm stretched as far as it could go to keep hold of His grip. We were on a desert road, and I could see the cityscape in the far distance. I heard His voice say, "All you have to do is hold my hand. Don't let go. I am doing all the leading and watching. You just hold on and enjoy the journey."

I will never forget that picture. All He was asking me to do was to hold onto Him.

These are a few of many journal entries, seeking God for our financial needs. The following were from 2007, the year after Brew's eye injury. He was unable to work, and the real estate market was crashing.

2/16/07 - $300 was in an envelope and left on our front porch! We are trusting Jesus for our provision. Praise God! The envelope was typed and it said "The Briggs Family," nothing else. $300.00 cash!

2/22/07 - Someone gave us $500. She said the Lord told her to give it this week. This was the week I wrote out ALL our bills by faith. We needed it so badly. Thank you, Jesus. Someone else gave me a Costco gift card for $150. Brew and I both needed gas. Thank you, Lord Jesus, for supplying all our needs.

3/7/2007 - We continue in prayer for this month's bills. We just got word that the Lord has put it on two brothers' hearts to give us $2,000. Praise God! He is providing all of our needs in His riches and glory. The Lord gave me Psalm 66 today. He is refining us and rebuilding us. He is decreasing us that He may increase.

3/30/07 - I got a refund check for $600 from an overpayment on my second mortgage. The LORD is faithful. Waiting and praying for escrows to close. Haven't closed yet. God knows our needs and He will supply. We received two gift cards for $25 each to Target and Henry's. Praise God! He is so good to us!

4/21/07 - We received a gift of $1,000! God continually pouring in. The LORD burdened someone's heart for us and sent $2,500 and a $500 gift card. Amazing! God is providing. He is sustaining. He is the LORD. My heart was pricked as He spoke to me through a sister, about how He provided manna to the children of Israel. They wanted something more and were getting greedy. I want to be thankful for His provision, even if it is not very tasty. It is daily bread to us. I am thankful. It is good. He will provide for us all our needs. He is a good Papa and Shepherd. Thank you, Jesus.

9/17/07 - The Lord is so faithful to give us a $500 gift from a lady at church. She said she had it in her purse for a month and kept forgetting to give it to me. Amazing!! We need that money badly!! The Lord is so good!

11/7/07 - We are down to 0 dollars and maxed out on overdraft. The LORD so faithfully provided through the sale of Brew's mom's home, and we will receive a check for $4,700. Just enough for this month: mortgage, tuition, bills. Plus, Brew made $300, and I made $300 cleaning a house. Praise God! He is faithful! The Lord is so sweet to us. I am slightly uneasy due to real estate having no guarantees as I have experienced. But I am going forward in faith. That is what the Lord does. He gives and takes away.

7/2//09 God is raising awareness in people to give. We only had a little bit in the bank. I asked the Lord for more money to be in the account. He sent someone to give us $4,000. Also, a lady sold her hair and bought $250 worth of diapers and formula for the storehouse. $80 was found in the pocket of a pair of shorts that were donated. We had to pay our food bank bill and rent. "Lord, help me let go and trust you more. Give me wisdom. I am feeling burdened, and I am needing you, only you. You build this house. Help me let it go and not worry about what others think or don't think. You are glorified in all of this or let it not be. Give me your wisdom, on how to operate this, or change it, or grow."

7/3/09 - Today we helped an Ethiopian man and his wife. They are new arrivals and found a room in a house with 10 other people. God *provided so many wonderful things for them today: a perfect bed, beautiful linens, a chair, a bookshelf, kitchen items, a TV, and a DVD player. They were overwhelmed and extremely grateful. They prayed for me that God may give His grace to "carry the people." They prayed to the Lord saying there are many problems, "God give her grace. Now we know you God are with us. You are a God of the desolate. You are the God of the needy. You are a God who answers the afflicted." This was his prayer of thanks after receiving so much good to start his life here.*

Not all testimonies were in journal entry form. Some of our favorite stories are ones that we tell and retell out loud, like the following testimonies:

One day on 38th Street, we were in great need of XL women's clothing. We had visitors that week from Intervarsity, and I encouraged all of us, "Let's pray right now for those clothes to come in." They thought it was a bit strange but agreed to pray. Within one hour of praying, a lady dropped off three large trash bags full of women's XL clothing. The visiting team of young college students was blown away by this simple request and answer to prayer. Their faith increased at that moment, seeing that God cares about the smallest needs.

Small things can become "big" when you require them, and one particular story stands out in this way. Not long after Cecilia started volunteering with Bridge of Hope, she declared that we needed a wagon to take donations from one part of the building to another. She didn't want a dinky red wagon, but something a little tougher that could move over gravel and dirt. "Let's pray for a wagon right now," I said in faith. At the time, Cece thought that was pushing it a bit with God. Does He care about such things? We prayed anyway and left it in God's hands.

About a week later, a friend came by in her trailer with a huge load of items that we needed. She said to me, "Sheri, I'm not sure if this would be of use to you, but would you want a wagon?" Would we ever! It was a new wagon with bigger wheels, exactly what we prayed for. This was a gift to us not only for the work we did but as a boost to our faith. We could believe God for everything, even a wagon!

In 2009, I met a girl who was 15 years old, pregnant, and homeless.

There was a group of about 12 kids that hung out in the town square by my house, and God put one of the girls in particular on my heart. I prayed and waited on God for what to do. One day, my girls and I were in the fabric store near the square when I asked a security guard about the kids. She told me they were all homeless and one was pregnant. I immediately gave her my card and asked her to give it to the girl who was pregnant. Within an hour, I got a call from the girl saying she was told to call me, and when we met that afternoon at Jack in the Box, I learned that she was five months pregnant and had not seen the doctor yet. But she had been to the pregnancy center when she was only two months pregnant and had decided to keep the baby. I told her I wanted to help and eventually took her back to the center to help her get the medical care she needed.

While she saw the doctor, I sat in the waiting room. "How do you know her?" the lady at the front desk asked me in a whisper. "We have been praying for her and the baby since we met them a few months ago. We didn't know what happened to her. We are so thankful to see she is here and still carrying the baby."

After four more months of being homeless and pregnant, this young girl decided to give the baby up for adoption. Within one week of her decision, we met with an attorney, and she picked a beautiful couple who had been waiting and praying for a baby for 15 years. The couple adopting the baby and I was all in the room with her when she gave birth. Since then, this precious young woman has been invited into the adopting family's life beautifully. She knows her daughter is so loved. It's truly a miracle.

At one point, we desperately needed blankets, pillows, and sheets for the families coming to us for these things. Out of the blue, we got a call from a fancy hotel in La Jolla who told us they were replacing all of their bedding and wanted to give us everything they had. We made three trips to the hotel that day, packing our cargo van full each time with high-end down comforters, duvet covers, pillows, and sheets. We barely had enough room to house all of it. That load blessed a lot of families that year!

One of my favorite stories comes from the very beginning. We were on 38th Street, where people from all over the world gathered together each week. We had three new arrivals–an older Bhutanese couple and their brother. One morning, they were trying to tell me what they needed through sign language and broken English. It felt like a long, frustrating game of charades. Suddenly, I had a thought and ran upstairs, grabbed an umbrella, and brought it back down. They started jumping up and down in sheer joy and hugging each other. Yes, they needed an umbrella, and we had one! That was a tender moment and describes our journey well. Often, the simplest things are the most important. It gets very hot in City Heights, and many people walk everywhere. An umbrella helps to fend off the heat in the summer, and the rain in the summer. No gift is too small or too basic to make an impact.

World Impact San Diego would go on weekly prayer walks around City Heights and noticed Bridge of Hope one day in 2011. We met and began talking and sharing about all the Lord was doing in the neighborhood. Jerry and Robbie Zeller and Cuco and Robyn Moya became our dear friends, prayer partners, ministry partners, and youth group leaders. They even started a Spanish-speaking church at Bridge of Hope that was a huge blessing to the community.

One year at our annual backpack drive, we got a call from our dear friend who helped us coordinate this event each year with churches and schools. One week before the event, they were very short on backpacks. The event was less than a week away, and we only had 100 backpacks, far less than what was typically needed. So, we began to pray.

The next day, our friend got a call from a lady she didn't know who was sending 100 backpacks to her house via Amazon. When we got to the Community Center that morning, children were lined up around the block waiting to get a backpack. I was told we had 350 backpacks to give. Every child that day left with a backpack. Not one child missed out, and not one backpack was left over.

At the end of the summer of 2013, I saw a church building and property in City Heights that I had never noticed before. This large and beautiful building was an old Ethiopian Episcopal church, located in a very rough area of City Heights–and it was available for rent. I knew I had to get inside and take a look at it. Once I entered, I realized that it was not only a church, but a hall, kitchen, enclosed courtyard, and two apartments. The wheels started turning. We had been renting a little studio on Fairmount Avenue for a single mother and her four children. The possibility of having two apartments onsite was significant, not to mention the potential of having a hall and courtyard.

Journal entry January 4, 2010- *I see a large community center. There, we can hold worship nights, eat, have fellowship, hold classes, play music, create a children and youth area, play games, do art, dance, host mentorship, and offer homework help. A place for people from all nations to come together and share with others. The walls are painted. There is furniture. It is warm and welcoming. A place to meet and be met. A light in a dark place. Hope in the City! An internship program–people coming and living and serving in the community. A place where all could come. The Spirit of the Lord welcomes all, and they are healed.*

Lord, what do we do? Do we keep 38th Street? Do we add another site? What do we do from here? Please confirm your vision with the provision. Thank you, Jesus. I surrender again to you.

(The vision I received and wrote down in my journal in January 2010 of a community center for Bridge of Hope came into being in 2013, and the building was exactly what the Lord had shown me.)

Saying "yes" to this opportunity took a giant leap of faith. It was a large, old property that would need significant renovation and repair . . . not to mention ongoing maintenance. Finally, it was a financial risk. The monthly rent was high, and we didn't have a ton of funding. And yet, we felt that God was leading us to jump in, feet first. So began our journey with the old Ethiopian Church on Trojan Avenue.

Once again, when it's God's will, it's His bill. Suddenly, churches throughout San Diego began to raise funds for us to clean and remodel the building. We had never heard of most of these churches and had no idea how they had heard of us. Yet, they were helping us to take care of repairs and changes throughout the property. Some of these churches even gave us their Christmas funds for the year. One church raised

$15,000 to replace the floors in the hall and kitchen. They were donating furniture, sending volunteers to help, and providing the funds to help us see our vision come to life. It wasn't just churches; a contracting company donated paint, and a restaurant donated tables and chairs.

Everything we needed was pouring in to convert the old church into a Bridge of Hope Community Center—complete with a center for worship and gathering, housing for visiting missions' teams, a basketball court, a tutoring club, and transitional housing for those who were facing homelessness and other crisis situations. When it was finished, we were able to have afternoon kid's clubs, weddings, funerals, church services on Sundays, and mid-week Bible studies. It was what God had shown me years before–exactly the vision I had journaled about.

We were becoming an umbrella for other ministries, and with all that we had been blessed with, we were able to bless new leaders and church planters. My prayer from years before was being answered; we were now the head and not the tail. We were giving, as God had so freely given to us. There was lasting fruit, lifelong connections between individuals, ministries, and churches, and a vision for the Kingdom of God that came forth from this place–and remain to this day.

One of our partners, Kaleo Missions, would bring teams from all over the country to Bridge of Hope to serve and run afternoon kids clubs all spring and summer. Now that we had space at the center, we had room for them to stay with us. The only problem was that we didn't have any showers. Around the time we realized this need, my dear friend Deanne with Rebuilding Together San Diego got in touch with us, asking if we had any building needs. Yes, we did! Rebuilding Together contracted plumbers, contractors, and electricians to install two showers on the property. Everything was paid for and perfect for what we needed–another amazing answer to prayer that allowed our facility to be useful and efficient for this beautiful partnership.

After getting the community center in 2013, we had to be able to transport kids for the youth group from the Fairmount location to the community center. We didn't have enough people to take them back and forth, so we began to pray for a van. Around this same time, a church reached out and said they wanted to bless Bridge of Hope with a grant of $5,000. We started looking for vans at that price point, but it was difficult to find something that didn't have super high mileage. One morning, I saw a 16-passenger bus on Craigslist. It had been operating at a senior citizen home, which meant it had to be serviced every thirty days and safety checked continually. It only had 72,000 miles on it and was in perfect shape. We bought it for $4,000 and used the remaining $1,000 to cover taxes, registration, and insurance.

Another wonderful story of provision: Many of our kids at Bridge of Hope never learned to swim, having been raised in refugee camps before arriving in the U.S. One day, the local Recreation Center pool reached out to us and asked if they could provide free swimming lessons for our kids in the spring and summer sessions. It was an amazing gift and necessity for our kids. Many children have learned how to swim over the years from that program.

During Christmas 2015, a local church chose Bridge of Hope to be the recipient of their big Christmas giving event. We had no idea how large this event was going to be and assumed we were just one of many charities chosen to be a recipient. We didn't realize we were the main event! The event was held in the convention center in downtown San Diego with live music, food, and fundraising…all for us! They raised $50,000 for Bridge of Hope, which included a furniture moving truck complete with a beautiful paint job with our logo, a rebranding, a website, and a complete makeover of the upstairs apartment at our Community Center.

At one point, we were getting low again in the bank account. I didn't ask anyone for money, but sought the Lord, laying the need before Him in detail and recording it in my journal. I simply asked others to pray, as I always do, though I am careful to never sound desperate or afraid. We had quite an overhead at this point with both buildings and only enough money in the bank to cover one more month of bills. I prayed and reminded the Lord that we had many people counting on us–including the families living at our center, the churches that met there, the youth, and the community in City

Heights. I reminded Him that I had encouraged many people over the years that *where God guides, He provides.*

Soon, I got a call from one of our donors after not hearing from him for a long time. He asked what was going on with Bridge of Hope and told me he was "sitting on a pile of God's money that needed to be used for the Kingdom." Those were his words, exactly. I sat in my truck and broke down in tears. He told me he was sending funds to Bridge of Hope and it would arrive in the next couple of days. Not in my wildest imagination could I have dreamed that he would send that amount. Opening the envelope, I fell to my knees, sobbing. Again, the Lord was saying to us through this gift, *I am with you, and I am holding your hand. Keep going.* There are no words to describe that moment, being with the Lord, feeling humbled, grateful, and in awe of His ever-present, unchanging love and provision.

One month, we had a family come to us who had just arrived from Cuba. The wife was eight months pregnant, and the whole family was homeless. They had met pastor Cuco, who is part of our Bridge of Hope family and held his church services at the Community Center. When they shared their situation with Cece and me, we waited on the Lord for His guidance. There are so many needs and only two apartments, but we knew that this was the family who was to move in next.

Very soon after they moved in, she had an emergency C section and gave birth to a baby boy who was born with serious complications. He had to stay in Children's Hospital for a few months and endure a few different surgeries. It was touch and go the whole time, but God knew what they were about to face and that they were going to need this apartment. Children's Hospital was only 10 minutes away from the center, which was important because they were going there every day for months. Providing this apartment and surrounding them with a family of love and faith for their child was God's care for this family. The surgeries and time spent in the hospital were a success, and their baby boy was released to come home. This family stayed with us for a few more months until God blessed the father with a job and a permanent place for them all to live.

Christmas 2014- A church that had blessed us in the past wanted to bless us again. They asked what our current needs were, and we told them we desperately needed a place to store all our furniture, a room that would be easy to access but that would keep furniture dry when it rains. We also needed to put in a concrete slab on our Fairmount property to eliminate the mud during the rainy seasons, as well as erect a new gate at the entrance of the building.

They were excited to jump right in and began raising funds and helping us apply for permits. They were determined to meet our needs and blessed us with a 40-foot Conex box for furniture storage, new concrete, and a beautiful, heavy-duty gate. Merry Christmas!

In the summer of 2015, National Charity League chose Bridge of Hope to be the recipient of their annual senior project. They put in a beautiful new yard with Astroturf, a play structure, retaining walls, new picnic tables, colorful umbrellas, outdoor furniture, and brightly colored pillows. This was a huge and wonderful gift to us and the community who gather there week after week. This was part of the fulfillment of the vision given and recorded in my journal in 2008:

9/1/08- God has given me a vision for a big house in the city. It will have a garden, fruit trees, and flowers. It will be colorful- benches, tables, and chairs. Beautiful for the children to see and visit. We will do arts and crafts, and music. There will be food, worship, prayer, and a swing set. It will be a colorful piece of heaven in the city.

Summer 2017, I was invited to a picnic of about 400 newly-arrived Syrian families. I was so excited to spend the day with friends and meet new families, but when I began my trek across the park, I stepped into a hole and twisted my ankle. Instant horrible pain shot through my leg. My ankle was broken. A Syrian gentleman whom I had met saw me fall and ran across the park, got his mother out of her wheelchair, and ran it back to me. He helped me get in the chair and wheeled me through the park and into the parking lot, where my daughter was waiting to take me to the hospital.

I was so sad. I hate when things slow me down. But here is the sweet part: in all the years we have accepted donations into Bridge of Hope, never once has a knee scooter been donated. I broke my ankle, and surprisingly, one shows up. I was able to scoot around Bridge of Hope and other places I needed to be, including my home. Random things appear *for such a time as this.* (Esther 4:14b)

In 2018, we were able to lease the property to the south of Bridge of Hope. It was nothing but a dirt lot with one small room that came with many challenges. We waited and prayed and recorded our hopes for the property in my prayer journal, asking God to bring in the funds and the hands and feet to make it possible. A year passed before Teen Volunteers in Action surprised us with a donation of $2,000. That made it possible to build a pantry for our food distribution on site. Another year passed and National Charity League informed us that we were chosen once again to be the recipient of their annual senior class project. By God's grace, Home Depot got involved in its efforts and vision for the property and provided an additional $5,000 worth of supplies and materials. We built a beautiful tutoring room and a whole new garden space.

11/2019 - Before Covid hit, the Lord spoke to both Cecelia and I at different times, this scripture, "For He will be like a tree planted by the water, that extends its roots by a stream, and does not fear when the heat comes; But its leaves will be green, And it will not be anxious in a year of drought, Nor cease to yield fruit." Jeremiah 17:8. NASB

This was a prophetic word that God revealed to us for what was coming. He was assuring us that our roots are deep in Him. He assured us by this word that in the day of trouble or famine, there would be no lack. We have been strong and have experienced an overabundance of provision and blessing pouring in during Covid. Bridge of Hope has become a giant shade tree, filled with fruit for many. We are blessed to be a blessing! There is such an abundance that leaders and pastors from all over San Diego and Mexico can come and take what they are needing to care for their flocks.

1/1/2020 As the Lord had been leading me to begin my grief support practice, I was seeking Him for who He was calling to manage and oversee the many moving parts of Bridge of Hope. God provided an incredible leader, Cecelia Brito, who had been volunteering with us for ten years, to become our Director of Operations. This was a huge answer to prayer.

May 2020 - After my son passed away in 2015, I began to get sick with what the doctors were calling, severe diverticulitis. I was in and out of the emergency room. I could only eat bone broth, sweet potatoes, potatoes, yogurt, and avocados. The surgeon was planning on removing 24 inches from my intestine, and at that point, I welcomed it. I was weak and had been in a lot of pain for three years, until one day, at our weekly food distribution, a woman of faith asked if she could pray for me. I had had lots of prayers over the last few years for this situation. She said a simple prayer, asking God to take the diverticulitis from me. That was the very last day I was sick, and as I write this, it has been two years since I have been sick. I eat everything I want to eat. I am completely healed. My doctor was in tears when she witnessed that I was healed. She said it was a miracle.

As much as we have witnessed the mighty and continual blessings, miracles, and provision of God, we were also a ministry that works hard. We are all about getting our hands dirty and doing whatever it takes to get the job done. If God is leading us, there is no job too small or too big for us to tackle. We all worked hard to pick up loads of everything from food and clothing to pots and pans and large furniture items. After items arrived at our site, they needed to be unloaded, organized, stocked and refilled. We did this over and over. That didn't even include the maintenance and care that goes into our properties and vehicles, all done by volunteers.

I have shared many miracle stories of God's provision. But I must add that a big part of our journey has been walking with others through their pain and sometimes what felt like unbearably challenging situations. Being in a community is both wonderful and difficult–just like life and love. At Bridge of Hope, we made ourselves available to those who were suffering. I've been blessed with many opportunities to pray and sit with children and adults who were dying and sat with parents who have lost their children. I've felt helpless in the face of PTSD, drug addiction, disease, poverty, war trauma, deportation of a parent or spouse, despair, mental illness, and hopelessness. I've advocated in schools, been in courtrooms to testify in cases against landlords, and worked with child protective services. I consider this a privilege and part of the miracle, but at times, it is overwhelming. I have often felt the Scripture, "I would have lost heart, unless I had believed That I would see the goodness of the LORD In the land of the living" (Psalm 27:13). NKJV

In the process of all this, I have learned a few things. One is to be there, present, and listening, to the one in front of me. I don't have answers, but I pray to the One who does, and I'll lead that person to the One who can bring lasting comfort and answers. I can do nothing more than be there and pray for that person. I have learned the power of pausing and listening and the power of caring and looking a person in the eye. I have learned the power of a smile, a hug, checking in with someone, and remembering a name. Never underestimate those things.

The Spirit of the Sovereign Lord is on me,
  because the Lord has anointed me
  to proclaim good news to the poor.
He has sent me to bind up the brokenhearted,
  to proclaim freedom for the captives
  and release from darkness for the prisoners,

to proclaim the year of the Lord's favor
  and the day of vengeance of our God,
to comfort all who mourn,

  and provide for those who grieve in Zion—
to bestow on them a crown of beauty
  instead of ashes,
the oil of joy
  instead of mourning,
and a garment of praise
  instead of a spirit of despair.
They will be called oaks of righteousness,
  a planting of the Lord
  for the display of his splendor.

They will rebuild the ancient ruins
  and restore the places long devastated;
they will renew the ruined cities
  that have been devastated for generations.

—Isaiah 61:1-4
(Imprinted on the fence behind our Fairmount Location)

Lightning Source UK Ltd.
Milton Keynes UK
UKHW022030090223
416682UK00015B/1875